PLAYS FOR PERFORMANCE

*A series designed for
contemporary production and study
Edited by
Nicholas Rudall and Bernard Sahlins*

BUDD SCHULBERG
WITH STAN SILVERMAN

On the
Waterfront

A Play

Ivan R. Dee
CHICAGO

ON THE WATERFRONT. Copyright © 2001 by Budd Schulberg and Stan Silverman. All rights reserved, including the right to reproduce this book or portions thereof in any form. For information, address: Ivan R. Dee, Publisher, 1332 North Halsted Street, Chicago 60622. Manufactured in the United States of America and printed on acid-free paper.

Library of Congress Cataloging-in-Publication Data:
Schulberg, Budd.
    On the waterfront / by Budd Schulberg ; with Stan
Silverman ; production notes by Kelly Patton.
        p.   cm. — (Plays for performance)
    The play.
        ISBN 1-56663-367-2 (acid-free paper) —
    ISBN 1-56663-368-0 (pbk. : acid-free paper)
    1. Stevedores—Drama.   2. New York (N.Y.)—Drama.
    3. Organized crime—Drama.   4. Catholic Church—
    Clergy—Drama.   I. Silverman, Stan.   II. Title.   III. Series.

PS3537.C7114 O5 2001
812'.52—dc21   00-047409

This play is dedicated
to the memory of
Father John Corridan, S.J.
"The Waterfront Priest"
and of Arthur Browne,
the irrepressible "Brownie"
who kept getting up to fight again

INTRODUCTION

by Budd Schulberg

On West 47th Street in New York I stand outside the Brooks Atkinson Theater, and there it is, on the marquee in big letters: "On the Waterfront." The play. Not the movie that surprised the director Elia Kazan and me when it overcame rejection by all the major studios to win a record number of Oscars and become a landmark film. But now in a legitimate theater only a ten-minute walk from the piers I had been drawn to after Kazan and I joined forces some fifty years earlier.

Malcolm Johnson's breakthrough exposé, "Crime on the Waterfront," in the long-lost *New York Sun* pointed us to our subject matter. Following Johnson's lead, I had gone down to St. Xavier's Church on West 16th Street to meet one of the most unforgettable characters of my life, the Waterfront Priest, Father John (Pete) Corridan. Tough, canny, fast-talking, chain-smoking and sometimes profane, he had become the champion of the dockworkers who were treated like convict labor by the racket-ridden International Longshoremen's Association, whose officers were literally recruited in Sing Sing and Dannemora.

I had walked into a brutal, inhuman world—just a few blocks from Sardi's. Rebel longshoremen daring to meet in the basement of St. Xavier's were set upon on their way out by racketeer union goons wielding baseball bats and steel pipes. But not a word appeared in any of the New York papers the next day.

Egged on by Father Corridan, I went to Turner Catledge, then the managing editor of the *New York Times*, and told him about the battle for control of the harbor that was going on from the Brooklyn docks to Hoboken. He invited me to write an article for the Sunday Magazine.

I came back with "Joe Docks, Forgotten Man of the Waterfront," a profile of the average longshoreman. There were some forty thousand of them, shaping up at dawn every morning, forming a human horseshoe around the hiring boss who picked them to work a four-hour shift according to his whims or according to the amount they were willing to kick back for the job—$2, $3, even $4 of the $2.27 per hour they were getting for the most dangerous work in America. "Joe Docks" described them as "forgotten men performing rugged, thankless jobs in a jungle of vice and violence where law and conventional safeguards never existed."

My three years of prowling the waterfront resulted in a screenplay that so excited Kazan he took it immediately to Darryl Zanuck at 20th Century Fox, who promptly threw it back at us with, "Who's going to give a damn about a bunch of sweaty longshoremen?"

Longshoremen, or workingmen in general, were not "in" in 1953, and they're still a rarity if not invisible in the movies of today. It was only with the intervention of a colorful, manipulative freebooter, the independent producer Sam Spiegel, that we managed to get the film made on a B budget and a thirty-five-day shooting schedule.

The Oscars, and the unexpected box-office success, were sweet revenge on the studios that had turned us down. But those years on the waterfront, including attendance at every one of the hearings held by the Waterfront Crime Commission, left me feeling that given the tight structure of a ninety-minute movie, we could tell only part of the story.

The film focused on Terry Malloy, a fringe hoodlum caught between obeisance to the mob and the gradual awakening of his own conscience, stirred by the innocence of Edie Doyle, the sister of the young rebel, whom Malloy had unwittingly helped to do in, and the prodding of the waterfront priest, now called Father Barry. What may strike many as a cliché—"If you do it to the least of Mine . . ."—becomes dangerous doctrine in Barry's mouth. It was dangerous for him to stand up to the waterfront mobsters because behind them was a complex support system, involving the church, big business, and city politics.

In our film the priest—memorably portrayed by Karl Malden—was a heroic figure. But there was no hint of the ordeal that his real-life counterpart had to endure in bucking the archdiocese.

The ideal film moves from sequence to sequence in a series of mounting climaxes. A novel has time to pause and wonder, time to put a Terry Malloy in proper perspective, to describe a social matrix of which Terry is totally unaware but one that is nonetheless driving him to put his life on the line. Choosing to do the novel through the eyes of "Father Pete Barry" gave me a vehicle for exploring his courageous challenge to church authority and describing his eventual banishment to an upstate, inland parish.

Despite what Sam Goldwyn was reputed to have said—"If you want to send a message, try Western Union"—I felt the message of my novel had been overwhelmed in the fame of the film and deserved to be heard more clearly.

Some fifteen years ago my lifelong friend and frequent collaborator, Stan Silverman, and I discussed still a third way of presenting the material: reinventing it as a play.

That the greatest natural harbor in the world was still held hostage by the mob exerted a nagging fascination on us. The cargo ships with their old-fashioned slings into the hold had given way to nine-hundred-foot container ships so high tech that two men could do the work of twenty. But credit the mob with resilience and resourcefulness. The Gambinos in Brooklyn and the Genoveses in Port Newark–Elizabeth weren't going to go away—not as long as billions of dollars' worth of cargo was moving in and out.

If the shape-up kickbacks were ancient history now, the high-level kickbacks from stevedores and shipping companies to crooked longshoremen union officials, and modern methods of corruption, were the old story in a new setting. No one on the inside, from the FBI to the United States attorneys to the district attorney to the computerized bi-state waterfront commissioners, doubts that despite their best efforts, the Five Families are still doing "very lovely" around the harbor.

It struck Stan Silverman and me that it was time to tell the rest of the story. And what better way than on the stage? The theater offers an opportunity to combine the drama of film with the subtext of a novel. But we had to find ways to dramatize the social and moral issues that there had been no time for in the movie and that were often expressed in interior monologues in the novel.

While the play includes scenes straight out of the movie and drawn directly from the novel, it also includes new ones that this third "Waterfront" demands.

8

The love story is still there, somewhat enlarged in fact, as we had more time to develop the relationship between Terry Malloy and Edie Doyle. While Terry's story remains, he shares virtually equal time with Father Barry, for whom, in the movie, there was not as much space as in the play, where he must come to terms with his own difficult choices and those of his critical superiors.

While there were worker-priests in France in the 1950s, and there have been priests speaking out for the impoverished peasantry of Latin America from the 1970s through the 1990s, the issue of liberation theology and the conflicts within the church about its current social role are sharpening every day.

The activism celebrated in our play may be new for the "X" Generation, which has often been accused of moral aphasia. Concern for one's fellow man or woman is considered old-fashioned and out of step in the era of get rich quick or starve on your own time and leave us Internet wunderkinds alone. Why should our overnight millions ease the pain of your unemployment or personal failure? some ask. Today's anthem, all too often, seems to be, "If you do it to the least of Mine, it's OK by me."

In the play, Terry Malloy expresses his philosophy of survival on the docks: "Do it to him before he does it to me!" It prompts Edie Doyle's question, "Isn't everyone a part of everyone else?" The answer to what seems a simplistic question goes to the heart of our modern malaise.

In the course of our play, Terry Malloy, the seemingly soulless street survivor, is forced to face up to the unfamiliar and inexorable demands of conscience, and the question: Where do we draw the line between naked self-interest and responsibility to our fellow beings?

Although the time of our play is still the mid-fifties, when crimes in fifty-seven varieties were shrugged off as the facts of life—and death—on the waterfront, the moral quandary that Terry and the waterfront priest face is the same one that the film and novel posed almost fifty years ago. Only now, in hindsight and, we hope, with foresight, are we able in this theatrical version to cut a lot closer to the bone.

On my way to the Brooks Atkinson a few years ago, I stopped to buy the morning papers and scanned them over a coffee-shop breakfast. The Javits Center, I read (not exactly with surprise), was a hive of labor racketeering. The waterfront, moved inland.

A carpenter's union official, who had been ousted for daring to speak up for union democracy, had been set on fire. The mayor was quoted as saying that if the Javits Center situation was not cleaned up, "It will go the way of the Port." And we all know what happened when Mr. Giuliani declared his intention to break the stranglehold of organized crime on the Fulton Fish Market. "They" burned part of it down.

The look has changed, the technology has changed, but the modus operandi of the old waterfront days is doing "very lovely" in the new waterfront days. And what is the waterfront, after all, if not a microcosm of the good-old-bad-old USA?

BUDD SCHULBERG

Long Island, New York
March 2001

10

BACKGROUND

The play takes place in the 1950s on and around the New York–New Jersey waterfront, which includes not only the piers but all the places around them—tenements and their rooftops, bars, riverfront streets, churches, cargo ships— where dockworkers and their families work, drink, worship, fight, live, and die.

CHARACTERS

WATERFRONT REPORTER*

TERRY MALLOY, a youthful ex-pug, cousin of Johnny Friendly

JOEY DOYLE, activist dockworker (doubles with BARTENDER)

MUTT, a drunken waterfront derelict

BARNEY
TRUCK } waterfront goons
LITTLE FRANKIE

CHARLEY (THE GENT) MALLOY, Terry's older brother

POP DOYLE
RUNTY NOLAN
MOOSE } veteran longshoremen
LUKE
TOMMY

JIMMY CONROY, Terry's teenage protégé

FATHER PETE BARRY, waterfront priest

JOHNNY FRIENDLY, "pistol local" union boss

BIG MAC, Johnny's hiring boss

"J.P." MORGAN, Johnny's loan shark
SKINS, Johnny's bag man (doubles with GLOVER)
EDIE DOYLE, Pop's daughter
GLOVER, a Crime Commission investigator
FATHER VINCENT O'MARA, senior priest in Fr. Barry's
    church
BARTENDER
LONGSHOREMEN
INTERROGATORS' VOICES (2)

*This play has been staged in two distinctly different ways: with fully realistic sets on Broadway or with stylized realism at the Cleveland Playhouse, and with minimal sets (a series of ramps on a virtually bare stage) at the Renegade Theater in Hoboken, New Jersey, and at Manhattan's Theater Row Theater. With the latter, to help set the scenes, a Waterfront Reporter was added as intermittent narrator. This role may be eliminated if sets are used, although the Theater Row version is preferred.

The Waterfront Reporter was suggested by director Kelly Patton, whose minimalist approach proved especially effective in the Hoboken and Theater Row productions, where actors were used for minimal scene changes and music was used for segue of scenes and cross-fading of lights.

Although the collaborators worked harmoniously in developing the play, they had a creative difference of opinion regarding the closing scenes. Mr. Silverman prefers to end the play at the end of Scene 12, adding only Father Barry's monologue which now opens Scene 13. Mr. Schulberg prefers including Scenes 13 and 14, essentially an Epilogue, if it is carefully and feelingly orchestrated.

On the Waterfront

ACT 1

Scene 1
A Riverfront Street

REPORTER: Did you know that only a few blocks west of here, just a short walk from Theater Row, you cross the boundary into another country, the New York waterfront—the greatest natural harbor in the world—host to the Cunard Line and the French luxury liners—and the hunting grounds of the pistol local—Four-forty-seven, The Skelly Mob. A no-man's land. The Wild East. Where hiring bosses are recruited in Sing Sing and Dannemora. Down there they tell you not to ask questions—if you want to stay healthy. But I'm a reporter. The docks are my beat. It's my job to ask questions. So I keep going down there looking for answers. OK, let's get to work. We're outside a rundown tenement, down the street from Johnny Friendly's Bar facing the piers. It's nightfall, in the mid 1950s.

(The cast files in. Terry Malloy enters last.)

MUTT: *(wanders through muttering a mournful song)* Tippi-tippi-tin, tippi-tin. . . . Tippi-tippi-tan, tippi-tan. . . .

TERRY: *(entering, calling up from street)* Hey Joey!

MUTT: Tippi-tippi-tan, tippi-tan. . . . Tippi-tippi-tan, tippi-tan. . . .

TERRY: Hey Joey! Hey Joey!

JOEY: *(calling down from rooftop)* Hey Terry! What do you want?

MUTT: Tippi-tippi-tin, tippi-tin. . . . Tippi-tippi-tan, tippi-tan. . . .

TERRY: *(reaching into windbreaker for live pigeon)* Look—He's one o' yers. I c'd tell from the band.

JOEY: Yeah? Must be Danny Boy. I been lookin' for 'im. Lost 'im in the last race.

TERRY: He followed my birds into my coop. I figured you'd want 'im back.

JOEY: I sure do. He's one of my best.

TERRY: Yeah, he's a nice bird. Wanna come down 'n' get 'im?

JOEY: Well, I don't know. I'm in a little hot water right now. Gotta watch myself with certain people—I guess you know who.

TERRY: Look, ya want yer bird back or don't you?

JOEY: Sure, only I'm not comin' down to get 'im. I'm stayin' off the streets these days, know what I mean?

TERRY: OK, so why don't I bring 'im up to yer coop?

JOEY: Yeah, I been checkin' on the little buggers an' there's nobody around. Thanks, Terry. See ya up here!

MUTT: Tippi-tippi-tin, tippi-tin. . . . Tippi-tippi-tan, tippi-tan. . . .

TERRY: *(running into Mutt)* What the hell—

MUTT: Jus' me, pal—jus' old Mutt. Got a dime fer a one-armed member of the Four-forty-seven?

TERRY: Fuck off!

MUTT: A dime fer a cuppa coffee . . . ?

TERRY: Don't gimme that coffee, ya juice-head!

MUTT: Terry Malloy. I shoulda known. You 'n' Joey grew up together. Only he's aces and you're a bum. *(exits)* Ya hear me, Terry? A bum! Tippi-tippi-tan, tippi-tan. . . . Tippi-tippi-tan, tippi-tan. . . .

REPORTER: *(Charley, Truck, and Skins enter)* Waiting for Terry outside Johnny Friendly's Bar are Charley *(the Gent)* Malloy and two enforcers, Truck and Barney.

CHARLEY: How did it go?

TERRY: Joey's up on the roof.

CHARLEY: The pigeon bit?

TERRY: Like you said, Charley—it worked. He's still up there.

CHARLEY: What did I tell ya? Nice goin', kid. Here's your sawbuck.

TRUCK: Dat brudder o' yers—thinkin' alla time.

BARNEY: All the time.

(Joey screams offstage ending with the thud of a body hitting the ground. Tommy, Luke, Moose, and Jimmy enter. An actor also enters and plays the body. Tommy places a jacket over the body.)

TRUCK: Waddaya know? Somebody fell offa roof.

17

BARNEY: Asshole thought he was gonna sing f'r the Crime Commission.

TRUCK: Bye, bye, birdie.

TERRY: You said they was only goin' to talk to him!

CHARLEY: Maybe he gave them an argument.

TERRY: I figured the worst they'd do is jus' lean on 'im a little. . . .

TRUCK: He's been givin' the boss a lot of trouble, kid.

TERRY: He wasn't a bad little fella, Joey.

CHARLEY: No, he wasn't.

TRUCK: Except for his mouth.

CHARLEY: Talkative.

TERRY: Wasn't a bad little fella. . . .

TRUCK: Maybe he could sing, but he couldn't fly.

BARNEY: Definitely. *(Barney and Truck exit)*

CHARLEY: How about a shot, kid? I'm buyin'.

TERRY: In a minute.

CHARLEY: Come on, kid. *(exits)*

RUNTY: *(entering)* Who is it?

TOMMY: Joey. Real bad.

RUNTY: Joey Doyle?

LUKE: All smashed up.

(Pop Doyle enters)

TOMMY: Yeah, don't let Pop—

POP: What's goin' on?

MOOSE: Pop, you better go on home . . .

RUNTY: *(holding Pop back)* Yeah, we'll take care o' things. . . .

POP: Lemme go! *(walks over to body)* Oh, Joey, Joey—I kept tellin' 'im, Don't say nuthin', keep quiet, you'll live longer . . .

RUNTY: Wasn't Joey's style, Pop. Never knuckled under to nobody.

MOOSE: We better get an ambulance—fast.

TOMMY: Ambulance ain't gonna help.

MOOSE: Kid, run down to Saint Tim's 'n' get one o' the priests. *(Jimmy exits)*

POP: If he oney lissened to me—stayed D 'n' D— He—he wouldn't be . . . Joey . . . Joey!

LUKE: Your boy had guts, Pop. Enough guts for a regiment.

RUNTY: A regular bravadeero. Strictly a stand-up guy.

POP: So put it on his tombstone! He gets a book in the pistol local and right away he's gonna be a hero! Gonna push thc mob off the docks single-handed. . . .

RUNTY: C'mon—let's go get a coupla shots in us.

POP: First I gotta call Edie, up at the school. *(starts to exit)* Edie an' Joey, they was like twins . . . *(exits)*

FATHER BARRY: *(enters followed by Joey)* The kid says there's been an accident.

TOMMY: Accident? Who's kiddin' who?

LUKE: That's what they always call it: an "accident."

MOOSE: Some accident!

19

FATHER BARRY: *(Father Barry kneels over the body and begins to administer Last Rites)* Susepe Domine/ Servum tuum/ancillam tuam/in locum sperandae sibi salvationis a misericordia tua/Amen.

Scene 2
Backroom of the Friendly Bar

(The boys are seated at a table and chairs, watching a fight on TV and shouting cheers and comments.)

BARNEY: Hey Terry—this ya gotta see!

TRUCK: Yeah, kid—Riley's makin' a bum outa Durazzo!

BARNEY: C'mon over and have a shot.

JOHNNY: *(Johnny Friendly enters)* Turn it off—them clowns can't fight. There's nobody tough anymore. *(to Terry)* Not like you, slugger. You coulda licked 'em both with one hand tied behind ya! How they hangin'? *(crosses to Terry and picks him up off chair)* Don't hit me now, don't hit me! *(sits in chair)*

MAC: Hey, boss—the cut from the shape-up. Skins turned it over t' me. Eight hunnert an' ninety-one men at three bucks a head makes twenty-six seventy-three.

JOHNNY: Not bad. *(to Charley)* Count it.

MAC: We get a banana boat tomorra. Pier Forty-six. If we pull a walkout, we might do very lovely with the shippers. I hear bananas go bad in a hurry.

JOHNNY: OK—ask ten G's. But make it look legit. Right, Charley?

CHARLEY: No problem. We tell the press we're just fighting for the rights of the men.

MAC: *(sings mockingly)* "Hold the fort, for we are coming—union men be strong . . . !"

JOHNNY: Shaddup! Where's Morgan? Where's that big banker o' mine?

MORGAN: *(enters)* Right here, boss.

JOHNNY: Well J.P., how's business?

MORGAN: Havin' trouble with Kelly again—he won't take no loans but Big Mac here puts him to work anyway.

MAC: He's my wife's nephew!

MORGAN: Screw it! He won't take no loans! How we gonna keep the men in line if you—

MAC: I got ta give 'im work! She'd moida me.

MORGAN: Tough tit! Here's the interest on the week, boss. Eighteen hunnert 'n' thirty-two.

JOHNNY: Hey Mac—count it. Oh, Skins—How'dja make out with the sheet metal?

SKINS: *(entering)* The new checker faked the receipt, an' two hours later the tin's sittin' in somebody's warehouse jus' like it belongs there.

JOHNNY: Who says it don't—if the price is right?

SKINS: Definitely. Forty-five bills.

JOHNNY: Hey Terry—front 'n' center. Count this.

TERRY: Aw, Johnny, ya know I don't like t' count. Gives me a headache.

21

JOHNNY: It's good for you. Develops your mind.

MAC: What mind?

TERRY: You're not so funny tonight, fat man. *(Terry takes a step toward Mac and vice versa)*

JOHNNY: Back up, Mac—I like the kid. Remember the night he took Farella at St. Nick's?

CHARLEY: We won a bundle.

JOHNNY: Real tough. A big try.

TERRY: Not a dent. Perfect.

JOHNNY: My favorite little cousin.

TERRY: Thirty-six—sev—ah, I lost the count.

JOHNNY: Skip it, Einstein. How come you never got no education like the rest of us?

MAC: Oney arithmetic he ever learned was hearin' the ref count over him—seven . . . eight . . . nine . . . ten!

TERRY: OK, fat man! *(Johnny stops them from fighting; Charley grabs Terry and pulls him back; and Mac backs up a few steps)*

JOHNNY: Charley, what gives with your brother tonight? He ain't himself.

CHARLEY: The Joey Doyle thing. You know how it is. Things like that—he exaggerates them. Too much Marquees of Queensbury. It softens 'em up.

JOHNNY: Listen, kid, I'm a soft touch too. Ask any rummy on the docks if Johnny Friendly ain't good for a fin anytime they put the arm on 'im. But my old lady raised us kids—ten of us—on a stinkin' watchman's pension. When I was sixteen

I hadda beg for work in the hold. I didn't work my way up outa there for nuthin'.

TERRY: I know, Johnny, I know. . . .

JOHNNY: Takin' over this local, Four-forty-seven, it took a little doin'. Some pretty tough fellas were in the way—Fisheye Hennesy an' Turkey Smith. They left me with this *(indicates scar on neck)*—See it?—to remember 'em by.

CHARLEY: He was holding his throat to keep the blood in and he still chased 'em into the street. They thought it was a dead man coming after them.

TRUCK: They was the dead men. Only they didn't know it yet.

JOHNNY: I know what's eatin' ya, kid. But I got two thousand members in my local, payin' five bucks a month dues—that's a hunnert an' twenny thousand a year legitimate—and when each one of 'm puts in two, three buck a day on toppa that, to make sure they work steady—well, you figure it out. An' that's just for openers. We got the fattest piers in the fattest harbor in the world—right, Charley?

CHARLEY: Everything that moves in or out, we take our cut. But there's plenty of problems and responsibilities. Believe me, whatever we make, we're entitled to it.

JOHNNY: We ain't robbin' pennies from the blind, kid. We're cuttin' ourselves in for five, six million a year just on our half-dozen piers. Ya don't think I'm gonna let anybody screw us outa that kind of a deal, do you? A deal I sweated and bled for—on a counta one lousy little cheese-eater, that Doyle

23

bum, who goes around agitatin' against us an squealin' on Johnny Friendly to that fuckin' Crime Commission. Do you? Well?

TERRY: Sure, Johnny, sure. He had his nerve, givin' ya all that trouble. I jus' thought I shoulda been told what was comin' . . . I mean I jus . . .

CHARLEY: Johnny—I make it twenty-six twenty-three from the shape. Skins shorted us half a bill.

JOHNNY: *(to Skins)* You shorted us! Gimme!

(Truck kicks Skins and pushes him to Johnny. Barney gets up and assists in the squeeze on Skins.)

SKINS: I—I musta counted wrong, boss. I—

JOHNNY: Gimme, schlagoom! *(after Johnny gets money from Skins he chases him off)* Cocksucker! You come from Greenpernt? Go back t' Greenpernt. You don't work here no more. Cocksucker! *(to Terry)* Here, kid—half a bill. Go get your load on.

TERRY: Thanks, Johnny—I don't want it. I—

JOHNNY: Go on—a little present from your Uncle Johnny. And Mac, tomorra mornin' when you shape the men, put Terry in the loft. Number One. Every day. Just check in an' goof off on the coffee bags. OK matooze?

TERRY: Thanks, Johnny . . .

CHARLEY: Hundred bucks a week for doin nothin', kid. You got yaself a real friend here. Don't forget it. *(Terry exits)*

JOHNNY: Why should he forget it?

Scene 3
Doyle Parlor

The Doyle parlor consists of a few chairs.

(Edie enters, as does Runty with Moose, Tommy, and Pop singing in traditional "wake" fashion. They are carrying bottles and glasses. Pop sits morosely in a chair.)

ALL: *(singing)* And freely as we lift our heads,
we vow our blood to shed,
once and forever more to raise,
the green above the red.

And freely as we lift our heads,
we vow our blood to shed,
once and forever more to raise,
the green above the red.

TOMMY: Aah, how Joey loved that song!

RUNTY: And why not? 'Tis a fine, brave song. An' he was the bravest of the brave, God rest 'im.

MOOSE: Lord've mercy on 'im . . .

RUNTY: Well, here's to God, Ireland, and the present company. . . . And mud in the eye o' Johnny Friendly!

MOOSE: An' the big boys on toppa him!

EDIE: *(suddenly, turning toward them)* Who'd want to kill Joey?

POP: Edie!

EDIE: The best kid in the neighborhood. Not because I'm his sister—everybody loved him. Are you all deaf? Who'd want to kill Joey?

POP: Pray for 'im, Edie, but don't ask no questions. Fer yer own good. Because you won't get no answers.

EDIE: Who did it?

TOMMY: You know how many murders we get down here every year, Edie? Ten or twelve—every year.

POP: Yes, Edie—an' you know how many that makes since you was born? An' how many got solved?

RUNTY: Just two, girl—in eighteen years.

MOOSE: They find a fella in the river—they say he was drunk an' fell off the stringpiece. . . .

POP: Or a high-low backs into 'im . . . or a sling slips.

LUKE: There's a dozen different ways.

POP: There's more accidents on the docks than anywhere else in the country.

RUNTY: So the pistoleros help the accidents along a little bit.

EDIE: But the police—why don't they do something? Isn't it their job?

POP: Oh, sure it is—in the books you read up there in college. Try 'n' change it, an' all you'll get is a snootful of trouble.

EDIE: Trouble? Can there be any worse trouble? Joey is dead. He's dead . . . !

POP: *(to Edie)* I know—I know. I never told you, but I was like him once. That's how I got this *(pointing to old wound on leg)*—n' I learned me lesson. Not Joey, rest his soul. He wouldn't listen. God's will Edie. Ya can't fight God's will.

EDIE: God's will? God's will? Are you telling me God wanted Joey dead? *(exits)*

POP: Edie! *(the boys stop Pop from leaving, sit him in chair, and start singing again)*

ALL: And freely as we lift our heads,
we vow our blood to shed,
once and forever more to raise,
the green above the red.

Scene 4
On Stoop Outside Doyle Tenement

(Edie enters. After a few moments Father Barry enters.)

FATHER BARRY: Edie. I've come to say the Rosary for Joey. It's rough—he was the best. Always there for six o'clock Mass. We're all gonna miss him. How's your pa takin' it?

EDIE: He's taking it. Better than I am. He's more old-fashioned about it. He's thinking that before too long, he'll be seeing him in Heaven. But I—I have to live all these years without him. Maybe that's selfish, but—but . . . Pop is sad but I'm mad, Father. I won't take it! I won't!

FATHER BARRY: Child, I know, I know. . . .

EDIE: Joey—he called me every week . . . Joey and I, all we had was each other. . . . He didn't fall off that roof—he must have been pushed! You know that, don't you? Well, if you don't, you should! No offense, Father, but you should. You should!

FATHER BARRY: Easy, Edie. Easy now. It's a bad day for all of us. I can't give you the easy answers. But time and faith . . . time and faith are great healers.

EDIE: Time and faith! My brother's dead, murdered by beasts who spit in the face of God. And all you stand here talking about is "time and faith"!

FATHER BARRY: Edie! It may not be enough, but I do what I can.

EDIE: Are you sure, Father? Isn't there more you could do?

FATHER BARRY: I wish there were. All I can do is help the family. Pray with you . . . and try to ease the loss.

EDIE: Only God has the power to give life . . . or the right to take it away. Isn't that true, Father?

FATHER BARRY: Of course—I preach that every day.

EDIE: So if— if those animals take Joey's life, and the police and everybody else just turn their backs on it, isn't it up to you to do something about it? Not just preach about it?

FATHER BARRY: Edie . . . I feel for you . . . it's hard to find the words . . . but they're waiting for me upstairs. Look, why don't we talk later? I'm in the church whenever you need me.

EDIE: "In the church when I need you." Look at St. Paul—Ignatius—Francis Xavier. You think they hid in the church? Was there ever a saint who hid in the church?

(Father Barry pauses a moment, then exits)

EDIE: *(continuing)* Oh, Mother, Mother of God, help me!

Scene 5
Doyle Parlor

(Runty and Tommy are sleeping. Runty is snoring with a bottle on his stomach rising and falling with each breath. The bottle falls off, waking them up.)

RUNTY: Holy shit! What time is it, Tommy?

TOMMY: I don't know—I think it's daytime. I hocked my watch last week.

RUNTY: Omigod; the sun's up . . .

TOMMY: Then it's time to shape, dammit.

EDIE: *(enters carrying two mugs)* Good morning, boys. Here's some coffee—take it with you. That's what Joey used to do.

TOMMY: Hey thanks, Edie.

RUNTY: Yeah, girl. Take care o' yourself. *(Tommy and Runty exit, picking up blankets and bottles from floor)*

FATHER BARRY: *(enters)* Morning, Edie.

EDIE: Pop's gone down to the shape.

FATHER BARRY: It's you I came to see.

EDIE: You think I spoke out of turn last night, Father? Well maybe I did, I was so angry . . . I'm still angry!

29

FATHER BARRY: Those saints you threw in my face. . . .
They kept me up all night.

EDIE: They took chances. Nothing scared them, Father. Nothing stopped them.

FATHER BARRY: But I'm just a gravy-train rider in a turned-around collar? Is that what you think? Is it? *(pause)* I see the Sisters taught you not to lie.

EDIE: I don't want to think that about you—I know it's not right. But honestly, Father . . .

FATHER BARRY: Edie, you don't understand. I put in a sixteen-hour day every day—comforting the sick and praying with them . . . helping youngsters out of trouble, getting them back to school, into a job . . . hearing confessions . . . celebrating Mass . . .

EDIE: And presiding at funerals, like Joey's.

FATHER BARRY: Edie, what do you want me to do? Pin a badge on my cassock and track down whoever killed him?

EDIE: Father, have you ever heard about those worker-priests in France? I just wrote a paper on them. I called it "Putting the Church Back in the Streets."

FATHER BARRY: Edie, I know about those priests. But that's Marseilles, Bordeaux. This is New York, Jersey—it's not the same over here.

EDIE: Why not? People get hurt, they get killed here same as over there. But if Joey had been killed in Marseilles or Bordeaux, I just know those priests would be doing something about it.

FATHER BARRY: We have a different set-up on this waterfront. We have a monsignor who's the official

Chaplain of the Port. That's his title. So the whole waterfront is his turf. Nobody in a collar is even supposed to set foot on the docks without his permission.

EDIE: This monsignor—if he's the Chaplain of the Port, maybe I should go to him.

FATHER BARRY: I'm afraid you'd be wasting your time.

EDIE: Why?

FATHER BARRY: He's very good at communion breakfasts, and fund-raisers for the Knights of Columbus—but when it comes to the kind of help you're looking for . . .

EDIE: So where does that leave me, Father? If the monsignor's a waste of time, and you won't help me . . .

FATHER BARRY: I can't, Edie! Look, I haven't been in this parish very long, and I'm not one of your saints—I'm barely making it as a priest.

EDIE: That's your problem, Father. Joey's mine. He was trying to make things better for the men— that's why he was killed. I know that much. Pop always told me to stay away from the docks. But if I want to get to the bottom of this, maybe I have to go down there.

FATHER BARRY: Edie, I can't let you do that!

EDIE: No? Well, you can't stop me.

FATHER BARRY: You're not going down there alone!

EDIE: Then come with me.

FATHER BARRY: I just told you—there are certain rules . . . I've got to think about it.

EDIE: Don't think too long. *(takes coat from chair)*

FATHER BARRY: Edie, wait a minute!

EDIE: I'm going, Father! *(exits)*

FATHER BARRY: Then dammit, I have to go with you! *(exits)*

Scene 6
An Active Pier

Crates and boxes are strewn around the pier.

REPORTER: *(enters)* The only way to do my job covering the waterfront is to blend in with the men—the hundreds of dockworkers who have to shape-up every four hours looking for a nod from the hiring boss—who's got the power of life and death over them—with at least four to five men shaping-up for every one picked. If I took out a notebook, or looked like a reporter, it'd be my last day on the job.

(Tommy and Runty enter)

MOOSE: Hey, what time did you get home?

TOMMY: What home?

LUKE: You was there all night?

RUNTY: I think I'm still there.

MOOSE: Too much o' Pop's good Irish whiskey!

TOMMY: And everythin' else in the house!

(Terry ambles past)

RUNTY: Hey guys, waddya think of this privileged character? Don't have ta shape-up no more.

MOOSE: Got yaself a soft touch in the loft, huh?

TERRY: Who says?

RUNTY: Waterfront Western Union.

TOMMY: You're doin' lovely, Terry—very lovely.

TERRY: Up yours!

MOOSE: My, ain't we touchy today?

LUKE: Why doncha lay off the kid, boys? Can't ya see how hard he's workin'?

TERRY: Fuck off, alla you!

POP: *(entering, carrying a windbreaker, and tossing it to Runty)* Joey's windbreaker. Wear it, Runty. Yours is more fulla holes than our union contract.

RUNTY: Thanks, Pop ... it's an honor but go home now. Everybody who works today is chippin' in fer ya.

POP: Look, boys, nobody's passin' the box fer me. I'm gonna shape. Who d'ya think's gonna pay fer the funeral—Johnny Friendly and Charley the Gent?

TRUCK: Hey, watch it! Better not dump on the boss!

RUNTY: You crazy? Who'd do a thing like that? Pop here was just tellin' us how thankful we should be to Johnny Friendly fer bein' such a pisser of a labor leader—an' doin' so much t' improve our workin' condition.

TRUCK: Don't you get wise, now!

POP: Wise? If he was wise he wouldn't be a long-shoreman for thirty years and poorer now than when he started.

LUKE: Like it is, brother—like it is!

MORGAN: *(entering)* Condolences, Pop. How ya fixed fer cabbage this mornin'?

RUNTY: Oh, me an' my pals 're just rollin' in the stuff, J.P.

TOMMY: We only work down here for a hobby.

MOOSE: Haw, haw, haw—that's a good one!

MORGAN: You'll be needin' a few dollars fer yer extras, won't you, Pop? You're three weeks behind on the last fifty, but I'm willin' to take a chance.

RUNTY: Some chance—at twenty percent a week!

LUKE: An' if he don't borrow, he don't work.

MORGAN: You'll work.

POP: I oughta belt you one, J.P.

MORGAN: Raise a hand t' me, an'—

RUNTY: An' you'll tell Johnny Friendly.

MORGAN: You'd be off the pier for good.

POP: All right, J.P., slip me a bill—and may you rot in hell.

MORGAN: When I'm dead 'n' gone you'll know what a friend I was.

RUNTY: Drop dead now, why don't you—so we c'n know it right away?

MORGAN: Condolences. *(exits. Pop sits on crate)*

34

GLOVER: *(enters)* Do any of you men know Terry Malloy?

TOMMY: Malloy, now? Never heard of him.

MOOSE: Me neither.

GLOVER: Hey—you're Terry Malloy!

TERRY: What about it?

GLOVER: Didn't I see you at the Garden three, four years ago with a fella named Wilson?

TERRY: *(bristles at the question)* Yeah. Wilson. I boxed Wilson.

GLOVER: I thought you were going to take him that night. You won the early rounds but . . .

TERRY: Okay, okay—without the bullshit. Waddaya want? *(Glover pulls out his ID)* Waterfront—Crime—Commission . . . ? What's that?

GLOVER: We're getting ready to hold hearings on mob control of the waterfront. Including your own local, Four-forty-seven—Michael J. Skelly, President.

TERRY: Who?

GLOVER: Better known as Johnny Friendly.

TERRY: I don't know nuthin'.

GLOVER: There's talk that you were one of the last people to see Joey Doyle alive.

TERRY: I still don't know nuthin'.

GLOVER: You're not accused of anything, Mr. Malloy. We just want to ask you a few things about people you may know.

TERRY: People I—you mean, sing for you? Get outa here before I—

GLOVER: I wouldn't advise that—unless you want to be booked for assaulting an officer of the law.

TERRY: Listen, I don't know nuthin', I didn't see nuthin', I ain't sayin' nuthin'. So why don't ya stop fuckin' me over?

GLOVER: All right, Mr. Malloy, you have a right to remain silent, if that's your choice. But the public has a right to know the facts too. I'll see you again.

TERRY: Never'll be much too soon.

GLOVER: Take it easy, kid. *(exits)*

TERRY: How about that joker—takin' me fer a pigeon!

TOMMY: Gimme the names. I'll write 'em down in me little book.

TERRY: One more word 'n' I'd a belted 'im, badge or no badge!

(Mac enters with a box, blowing a whistle. Everyone rushes to him)

REPORTER: *(standing on a crate)* Mac, the hiring boss, mounts a crate for the shape-up!

MAC: I got tabs here fer a hunnerd banana carriers. *(men are ad libbing and pushing at him)*

RUNTY: Bananas. Bananas! One o' these days me ship's comin' in from Ireland, God love 'er, loaded to the gunnels with sweet Irish whiskey!

POP: Runty me boy, yer dreamin' again.

36

MAC: *(blowing whistle again)* The following men report to the loft—Malloy—Hendricks—Krajowski.

RUNTY: *(as they go)* Don't work too hard! *(others laugh)*

MAC: Now the hunnerd banana carriers. *(The men begin to ad lib and push at Mac. Father Barry and Edie enter.)* Don't crowd me! Stand back!

MOOSE: Mac—I'll give two bucks for the job!

OTHERS Three, Mac—three! I give four! C'mon, Mac . . .

MAC: No shovin'! Or nobody gets nuthin'! *(pushes Tommy)*

FATHER BARRY: *(appalled)* Hey—what's going on here?

LUKE: C'mon, Mac, gimme a break—I need a day bad. Real bad!

MAC: Back off, Sambo! *(shoves Luke back into Barney)*

FATHER BARRY: What did you call him? Who do you think you are?

MAC: You're off limits, padre.

FATHER BARRY: Am I? Am I?

MAC: Damn right!

EDIE: *(crosses to Mac, Father Barry restrains her)* What have you got in the box?

MAC: Work tabs, nosy. You wanna work, ya gotta have one of these. No tickee, no washee.

FATHER BARRY: And you have a tab for every man here?

MAC: You crazy?

FATHER BARRY: Then who decides who gets one?

37

MAC: You're lookin' at 'im, padre. Now go back to ya church. You run your show—I run mine! *(the men start to ad lib and push at Mac again)* Back, ya fuckers—back! *(Flailing out at them. Slow motion begins.)*

REPORTER: I made mental notes on what was going on, so I could file it later. *(each action described takes place onstage)* Shoving Moose back, Mac is jostled and almost knocked from his perch. Luke reaches in and knocks the box of tabs from Mac's hand. The men scramble for the tabs on the ground.

MAC: Barney! Truck!

REPORTER: Runty Nolan grabs a tab and has to defend it against Truck. Pop Doyle grabs a tab and pays the price with a shot on the nose.

TOMMY: Hey Terry—grab one for me!

REPORTER: Pop's got to have that tab, and the job that goes with it, but Terry's too fast for him. *(Pop reaches for a tab. Terry steps on it and shoves Pop. He sits on a crate, and regular motion returns. Mac exits, and Barney and Truck take their places again.)*

EDIE: *(to Terry)* Give me that! It belongs to Pop. He saw it first!

TERRY: Oh, with all them muscles, I thought you was comin' to work.

EDIE: Give it to me! My Pop's job—

TERRY: What makes him so special?

EDIE: None of your business.

TERRY: Things're lookin' up on the docks, huh, Tommy?

TOMMY: Don't you recognize her, dopey? She's Edie Doyle.

TERRY: Joey's . . . You're his . . .

EDIE: Sister? Yes I am.

TERRY: You don't wanna lug bananas t'day anyway, do ya, Tommy? I'll make it up t'ya. Here ya go, muscles. Nice wrastlin' with ya.

EDIE: Pop—you're hurt!

POP: Naa—just the beak. It's been busted before.

EDIE: *(handing him the tab)* Here—I got it for you.

POP: OK, I can use it. Now go back to the Sisters where you belong! *(to Father Barry)* And you, Father, I'm surprised at ya! Bringin' Edie down here—a place like this. . . . She's a decent girl!

FATHER BARRY: I tried to stop her—but by God, I'm beginning to think she was right!

MAC: *(enters)* Hey, Doyle—you got a tab?

POP: Yeah!

MAC: Then get yer ass in here! Number three gang, number one hatch. Pronto!

POP: Go home, Edie. I mean it—now! Fer God's sake, go! *(exits, followed by Runty)*

EDIE: All right, Pop—all right! *(exits)*

FATHER BARRY: Edie—I'll see you later.

MAC: That's all, fellas. On yer way. Come back tomorra. *(Mac and Terry exit)*

REPORTER: I was on my way out of there, when I noticed the priest was stickin' around. I figured I would too.

FATHER BARRY: I can't believe this! What do you fellas do now? C'mon—what're you gonna do?

LUKE: Like the man says. Come back tomorra.

FATHER BARRY: You mean—you just take it like this?

MOOSE: Five straight mornin's I'm standin' here an' the bum looks right through me. There's always a couple hunnerd left in the street waiting fer work.

TOMMY: *(eyes the goons)* Shhh! Look who's over there.

FATHER BARRY: And there's nothing you can do? How about your union?

MOOSE: Don't ya know how a pistol local works, Father? Get up in a meetin', make a motion, the lights go out.

TOMMY: Three guys talk on a corner, an' Johnny's boys—they break it up.

FATHER BARRY: But the auto-workers—the garment-workers—steel—they got rid of those bums years ago!

LUKE: Father, this is the waterfront. Here the bums get rid of us. Like Joe—*(Barney crosses to Father Barry. Truck crosses to Tommy and Moose.)*

TOMMY: Sshhh! Let's move it!

BARNEY: Hey, what is this, a church picnic? Now fuck off! 'Scuse me, Father. *(exits)*

FATHER BARRY: What's he supposed to be?

TOMMY: One of our business agents. Johnny Friendly "elected" 'im.

MOOSE: That's how it's been ever since Johnny an' his pistoleros moved in on us.

40

TOMMY: Show me one place where it's even safe to talk.

LUKE: We tried the American Legion Hall—but they came right in behind us.

TOMMY: Then we tried the Knights o' Columbus. Forget it.

MOOSE: Even tried an abandoned pier—that was Joey's idea. Only the cowboys got wise and they was all over us.

FATHER BARRY: Use the church.

LUKE: What are you saying, Father?

FATHER BARRY: You can use St. Timothy's. The basement. OK?

MOOSE: Father—ya know what you're lettin' yerself in fer?

TOMMY: How will it go down with your boss?

LUKE: Yeah—how about Father Vincent?

MOOSE: And how 'bout the fat cats on toppa Johnny Friendly? They leave a lot o' cabbage on the collection plates.

FATHER BARRY: Good question, boys—I just wish I had the answers.

LUKE: Do we use the basement or don't we?

TOMMY: Do we or don't we?

FATHER BARRY: Use it. Seven o'clock tonight. OK?

MOOSE: Good with me.

LUKE: OK here.

TOMMY: You got it. *(Father Barry, Luke, Moose, and Tommy exit. Barney and Truck exit, and Terry enters.*

Scene 7
A Loft in the Pier

(Charley enters and nudges Terry who has fallen asleep on the coffee bags)

TERRY: Hey Charley—what's up?

CHARLEY: That's precisely what you're going to find out for us kid: What's up.

TERRY: Huh?

CHARLEY: Just saw Father Barry waltzing down the street with some redhots who might give Cousin Johnny a little trouble. Tommy, Moose, and that big spade. You know 'em, huh?

TERRY: I know 'em. So what?

CHARLEY: So what are they doing with Father Barry and vicey-versey?

TERRY: How would I know?

CHARLEY: You don't know yet—none of us do but they're getting up a meeting at St. Timothy's tonight—so you gotta use your eyes and ears real good.

TERRY: Aw, Charley. I don't wanna go in no church.

CHARLEY: *(ignoring this)* When you find out, you tell me, OK? Might be nothing, of course. But if it's something, kid, you fill me in—immediately. Don't stop for a beer.

TERRY: Ya want me to go on the earie fer ya? I dunno, Charley.

CHARLEY: What's to know?

TERRY: I'd be stoolin', Charley. Like a fuckin' pigeon.

CHARLEY: Lemme explain you somethin', kid. Stoolin' is when you rat on your friends, the guys you're with. When Johnny wants a favor, Terry, don't try to figure it out. Just do it. Join the congregation. *(exits)*

Scene 8
Father Barry's Study and the Church Basement

Father Barry's study contains a few tables and chairs. A telephone is set on one of the tables.

FATHER VINCENT: *(entering, to phone)* Timothy's—Father Vincent. Yes, there's going to be a meeting tonight. Seven o'clock, as far as I know. . . . No, I don't know where Father Barry is—haven't seen him all day. Can I give him a message. Hello— hello? *(hangs up phone and starts to exit when phone rings again, to phone)* St. Timothy's—Father Vincent. Hello—hello—? *(Father Barry enters with folder)* Where have you been? That meeting of yours is supposed to start in ten minutes.

FATHER BARRY: I've had a helluva day, Vince. Been chasing my tail from Brooklyn to Hoboken and down the South Street docks. Do you know how many longshoremen they've got on the books? Over forty thousand—fighting for maybe twenty thousand jobs! And I mean fighting!

FATHER VINCENT: Pete—who've you been talking to?

FATHER BARRY: Everybody! Newspaper guys—homicide cops—men from three different locals . . . they were afraid to talk but they steered me to the Waterfront Crime Commission. *(to Father Vincent; hands him folder)* I got their preliminary report—confidential. You have to read it!

FATHER VINCENT: Did you get an OK from Father Dowling before you got into all of this?

FATHER BARRY: Well, so far he hasn't said no.

FATHER VINCENT: So far. *(to Father Barry; hands him folder)* Pete, I've been here twenty years. You've been here six months. I'll grant things in this parish aren't perfect, but—

FATHER BARRY: Perfect? Hey look, Vince, I'll admit I've been damn-near deaf-dumb-and-blind to what's been going on down at the docks, but—I've been reading this stuff on the ferry, in the subways, the waiting-rooms—and what's it say? The locals aren't real unions, they're simply fronts for the mob—working against the men instead of for 'em. It's a conspiracy, Vince—

FATHER VINCENT: Ancient history.

FATHER BARRY: My God, so we just let it go on for another twenty years? The shipping companies, the stevedore companies, the I.L.A. bosses—They created this mess, and they keep it that way. They like it that way!

FATHER VINCENT: Look, Pete, I know there's a problem, and it's been there for a long time, but—

FATHER BARRY: But what? There's nothing we can do about it? We just let it go on growing like a cancer for another twenty years?

FATHER VINCENT: You think I don't feel for the men and their families? You know how many times I've run collections to put food on the table when kids're going hungry?

FATHER BARRY: Sure, Vince, I know—I've done it myself—but I'm starting to feel it's all too little, too late. I tell you, the men coming in tonight are being pushed around on the docks—and every so often being pushed off the docks. Like Joey Doyle. You must've known him. His sister says he was an altar boy here.

FATHER VINCENT: I remember, I remember.

FATHER BARRY: So we've got to help them. Not just to get to heaven—to stay alive!

FATHER VINCENT: That's exactly the point! The way you're talking, you're going to get them killed— some of them, anyway.

FATHER BARRY: They say it's better to die on your feet than live on your knees.

FATHER VINCENT: *(to Father Barry)* Pete, Pete—you've got a lot of brains, no telling how far you could go—monsignor, bishop even. I mean it. But if all of a sudden you start leading these people into open rebellion—

FATHER BARRY: C'mon, Vince! All I'm gonna do is ask 'em to act like Christians—members of the Mystical Body of Christ—and start treating each other that way. Have you any problem with that?

FATHER VINCENT: Damn right I have!—just don't agitate them, Pete! You could lose more than you could possibly gain. It's so much more complicated than you realize. I'm not just talking church politics—there's city politics, bi-state politics—and on top of the heap, calling the shots, are the Mister Bigs who use mayors and monsignors like office boys. You're up against so many different forces—so many factions . . .

FATHER BARRY: Vince . . . Vince, doesn't it bother you that some of these "factions" are getting away with murder . . . while we go on spouting Latin and swinging our smoke-pots?

FATHER VINCENT: Pete, you've got to slow down—slow down a little!

FATHER BARRY: Why! So things can go on just like they've been going—from bad to worse? No, thanks! *(takes folder and exits)*

(Father Vincent exits. Tommy, Moose, Runty, Luke, and Edie each enter separately and sit down. The Reporter remains standing.)

FATHER BARRY: *(enters)* Good evening, men—Edie. Frankly, I was hoping there'd be more of you here.

MOOSE: Well, Father, for every one of us who had the guts to show up, we know at least ten, maybe twenty, who feel the same way we do about what's goin' on—

TOMMY: Only they're too scared to speak up or show their faces . . .

LUKE: Or even come to a meetin' in a church!

FATHER BARRY: Well, the Romans found out what a handful could do, if it's the right handful—and I'd say the same goes for you.

EDIE: Yes, Father, we know what that handful did— Peter and Paul and the rest of them—they turned their world upside down. But this handful—What can we do? Have you any ideas?

FATHER BARRY: Well, I'm just a potato-eater, but it seems to me the only way you can make things better down here, like Joey Doyle was trying to do, is to take your local back from the mob. And there's just one way to do that—stop lettin' 'em get away with murder.

RUNTY: *(sarcastically)* Great idea, Father. Why don't we do that?

TOMMY: Easy to say, Father—easy to say.

FATHER BARRY: But hard to do? Maybe—but there's a new element in the picture: The Waterfront Crime Commission. I've been to see them— they're getting ready to hold hearings that maybe could turn things around down here—

RUNTY: Don't make me laugh, Father.

EDIE: You hear that, Tommy?

FATHER BARRY: —provided they can get guys like you to work with them.

LUKE: Work with 'em? How, Father—how?

FATHER BARRY: By telling them everything you know about what you're up against. You don't have to tell 'em what happened to Joey Doyle or why it happened—they know that. All they need is the

47

who. Who killed Joey Doyle? *(silence)* No one's got
a lead on who killed Joey Doyle? I've got a hunch
every one of you could tell them something about
it. *(silence)* Then answer this one. How can we protect his murderers with our silence and still call
ourselves Christians?

EDIE: Tommy—you were Joey's best friend. How can
you just sit there and not say anything? *(Tommy is
silent)* Tommy, I'm talking to you.

TOMMY: I'll always think of him as my best friend,
Edie—he was like my own brother. But what the
Father's talking about, I don't know. It's too—

(Terry enters)

RUNTY: Who asked him here?

FATHER BARRY: Have a seat. We're trying to find out
about Joey Doyle. Maybe you can help.

RUNTY: The brother o' Charley the Gent? He'll help
us to the bottom o' the river!

TERRY: Keep Charley outa this.

RUNTY: Ya don't think he'd be—helpful?

TERRY: Go ask him, why don't ya? Ask 'im yaself.

FATHER BARRY: All right, all right! Now let's get back
to Joey Doyle. Don't dummy-up on me, guys.
Come on. *(Father Vincent enters)* You know who the
pistols are, you see 'em on the docks every day.
Are you going to help the Crime Commission
crack this thing? Or are you gonna keep still till
they cut you down one by one? *(silence)*

FATHER VINCENT: Pete, you're out of line.

FATHER BARRY: *(to the men)* Are you? Are you? How
about you, Runty?

48

RUNTY: Father, one thing you gotta understand. On the docks, we've always been D 'n' D. Deef 'n' Dumb. Somethin' c'n happen right in front of our noses an' we don't see nuthin'. You know what I mean? No matter how much we hate the torpedoes, we don't rat.

FATHER BARRY: Boys—get smart. Here's your chance to get the facts to the public. Testifyin' for what you know is right against what you know is wrong. What's "ratting" to them is telling the truth for you. Can't you see that? *(silence)* Huh? Huh?

FATHER VINCENT: I think you'll agree, Father—we've done about all we can do at this time. So I'd like to close with a few words from St. Matthew. "Come unto Me, all ye who are heavy laden, and—"

(Sounds of brick breaking basement window and pounding of baseball bats offstage. Everyone jumps to their feet.)

RUNTY: That's our friends.

FATHER VINCENT: I told you, Pete—I told you! Now I have to call the police! Do you know what that window cost?

FATHER BARRY: *(picking up brick)* We must be on the right track or they wouldn't be sendin' us this Valentine. There's a back way out, through the courtyard. Better go home in pairs. *(Tommy and Luke exit. The Reporter hides)* If they lay a hand on any of you I'll see they go to jail—I swear it! *(Father Barry exits and Edie begins to follow)*

MOOSE: Fat chance.

RUNTY: I'm walkin' out the front way. Let 'em have me. I don't hide from them bums. *(Runty exits fol-*

lowed by Moose. Edie turns to follow them out and is stopped by Terry.)

TERRY: No—the back way.

EDIE: Why should I go with you?

TERRY: Dincha hear what the Father said? We gotta go out the back. I know the way.

EDIE: I'm not going anywhere with you!

TERRY: *(grabbing her)* Oh f' Chri'sake come on!

EDIE: Take your hands off me!

TERRY: Look, stupid, we got no time to crap around!

EDIE: Don't you dare talk to me like that!

(Runty and Moose enter. Runty is holding his head.)

TERRY: I'm not talkin', I'm takin' you outa—

EDIE: Oh my God . . . !

TERRY: Now d'ya get the picture? Let's go! *(Terry and Edie exit. Father Barry enters.)*

FATHER BARRY: How bad is it?

MOOSE: Johnny's boys was layin' for us. With baseball bats. They was usin' his head fer the baseball!

RUNTY: Hell of a thing t' happen to a ladies' man.

FATHER BARRY: Nice fellas.

RUNTY: Oh, how I'd love to fix them bastids! But . . .

FATHER BARRY: But it still has to be D 'n' D? It'd still be "ratting"?

(Father Vincent enters)

RUNTY: Father—are you on the level?

50

FATHER BARRY: What do you think?

RUNTY: Don't get sore, Father—but we've seen an awful lot o' phonies on the waterfront. Mayors. Police Commissioners. D.A.'s . . .

MOOSE: Even some priests.

RUNTY: The whole stinkin' high-ocracy.

FATHER BARRY: I know.

RUNTY: If I stick my neck out, and they chop it off—

MOOSE: Like they done to Joey!

RUNTY: Will that be the end of it, Father? Or are ya ready t' go all the way?

FATHER BARRY: OK, Runty—that's a fair question . . .

FATHER VINCENT: Pete—I'm warning you . . . !

FATHER BARRY: And here's my answer: I'll go down the line—believe me.

MOOSE: Baseball bats—that's just a warning. Next time . . .

RUNTY: An' that includes you, Father—collar or no collar.

FATHER BARRY: Stick your neck out, and I'll stick mine.

FATHER VINCENT: Pete, you don't know what you're saying.

RUNTY: Right down to the wire?

FATHER BARRY: So help me God. Your move, good lookin'.

MOOSE: Runty, let's get out of here!

RUNTY: Hell, I've had my fun—I've drunk my fill an' tickled my share o' fillies—I'm on borried time. OK, Father—let's try it your way.

FATHER BARRY: Here we go, Runty. Here we go.

FATHER VINCENT: Damn fools!

Scene 9
A Riverfront Street

MUTT: *(wandering through)* Tippi-tippi-tin. . . . Tippi-tippi-tin. . . .

TERRY: OK, I think we lost 'em.

EDIE: Baseball bats!

TERRY: Yeah, they play pretty rough.

EDIE: Which side are you on?

TERRY: Me? I'm on my side—Terry Malloy's.

EDIE: I can make it home from here myself.

TERRY: I better see you get there.

MUTT: *(approaching, frightening Edie)* A dime. One thin dime for a cuppa coffee.

TERRY: That's a laugh, coffee. His belly ain't used to nuthin' but rotgut whiskey.

MUTT: One little dime you don't need? *(now recognizing her)* I know you—yer Edie Doyle. Yer brother—he was a saint. Only one ever tried to get me my compensation . . . for the arm I left on Pier Forty-one.

52

TERRY: *(taking Edie)* C'mon—let's get outa here.

MUTT: You remember, Terry. You was there the night Joey was—

TERRY: Aah, fer Chri'sake quit yer yappin'!

MUTT: You remember—ya bumped inta me when you was—

TERRY: *(to Mutt)* Yeah, yeah—here's a couple o' shots fer ya. Now beat it—go have yaself a ball.

MUTT: *(taking the money)* I can't believe it. A small fortune. Good luck, Edie. Lord've mercy on Joey. Ya can't buy me, Terry. You're still a bum! *(exits)*

TERRY: Look what's callin' me a bum.

EDIE: Hear what he said about Joey? Everybody loved him.

TERRY: Yeah.

EDIE: Did you know him very well?

TERRY: Everybody knew him. He got around.

EDIE: What did that—that poor man mean when he said you were there the night—

TERRY: Aah, he's a rum-dumb—he talks to himself—the joke of the neighborhood . . .

EDIE: Good night.

TERRY: Don't be afraid of me. I ain't gonna bite you. Don't they let ya walk with fellas where you've been?

EDIE: You know how the Sisters are.

TERRY: You trainin' t' be a nun? *(she laughs softly)* Ya know, ya got a real sweet laugh. Real sweet. Well, are ya?

53

EDIE: Training to become a nun? No, I'm going to a regular college—Marymount. It's just run by the nuns.

TERRY: An' you spend all yer time jus' learnin' stuff, huh?

EDIE: I want to be a teacher.

TERRY: A teacher! Pow! Y'know, I admire brains. Take m' brother Charley. He's very brainy. Very.

EDIE: It isn't brains. It's how you use them.

TERRY: Yeah. Yeah. I get your thought. Y'know, I seen you lotsa times before. Parochial school on Pulaski Street? Seven, eight years ago? Your hair come down in—

EDIE: In braids? That's right.

TERRY: Looked like two pieces o' rope. An' your teeth were—

EDIE: I know. I thought I'd never get those braces off.

TERRY: Kid, you were a mess!

EDIE: I can get home all right now.

TERRY: I was just kiddin'. The thought I'm tryin' t' get over t' ya is—you grew up very nice. Remember me from them days . . . ?

EDIE: The moment I saw you.

TERRY: Some people got faces that stick in your minds.

EDIE: I remember you were in trouble all the time.

TERRY: You said it. A wonder I wasn't punchy by the time I was twelve. The rulers those Sisters useta

54

whack me with! They thought they c'd beat an education into me. I foxed 'em.

EDIE: Maybe they just didn't know how to handle you.

TERRY: Yeah? How would you 'uv done it?

EDIE: With a little patience and kindness. You know what makes people mean and difficult? When nobody cares about them. *(Terry mimes playing a violin)* All right, make fun of me if you want to.

TERRY: "Patience an' kindness." What're you on, nose candy?

EDIE: What?

TERRY: What-what? Where you been the last five years? Outer space.

EDIE: When my mom died, Pop sent me to school up in Tarrytown. He was afraid with no one home I'd—get into bad company.

TERRY: Smart. Too many good-for-nuthins around here. All they got on their mind's a little beer, a little pool, a little nook—*(catching himself)* C'mon, I better get you home. *(pause)* Am I going to see you again?

EDIE: What for?

TERRY: I don't know. But am I?

EDIE: I really don't know. *(pause)* We're almost there. I'll see. Good night.

TERRY: It's been nice talkin' to you.

(Edie exits)

Scene 10
Edie's Bedroom

(Pop is packing a suitcase; Edie enters)

EDIE: Pop—what're you doing?

POP: I'm packin' you up—an' out. You're leavin' tonight.

EDIE: I'm not ready to go.

POP: Oh yes you are! Your bus ticket and some eatin' money. You're goin' back t' Marymount. T'night!

EDIE: No!

POP: No? Waddaya think me an' Joey pushed quarters into a cookie jar for, week after week, year after year? It was to keep you up there with the Sisters, an' t' keep you away from things like I just seen out the window—my own daughter arm-in-arm with Terry Malloy! You know who Terry Malloy is?

EDIE: The brother of Charley Malloy.

POP: Charley the Gent. Johnny Friendly's right-hand man! A butcher—in a camel's hair coat!

EDIE: And that makes Terry a butcher, too?

POP: It don't make him Little Lord Fauntleroy!

EDIE: Oh, I know he tries to act tough, Pop. But there's a look in his eyes . . .

POP: A look in his eyes? Jesus, Mary, 'n' Joseph, here we go again! You think he's one o' them strays ya was always draggin' home an' feeling sorry fer. Like the litter o' kittens ya had—the only one she wants t' keep has six toes and it's cockeyed to

56

boot. An' what about the crush you had on that little Abyssinian?

EDIE: He wasn't Abyssinian, Pop. Don't you remember? He was a—Assyrian.

POP: Six-toed cats. Assyrians, Abyssinians—it's the same difference. Well, I don't think this Terry Malloy is any six-toed cockeyed Assyrian—he's a bum. Charley and Johnny Friendly owned him when he was a fighter, and when they ring the bell he still comes out throwin' punches for 'em.

EDIE: He wants to see me again.

POP: See this arm? Two inches longer'n the other one. That's years of workin' an' sweatin'—liftin' an' swingin' a hook. An' every time I hefted a box or a coffee bag, I says to myself—this is for Edie, so she can be a teacher or somethin' decent!

EDIE: Pop . . .

POP: I promised your mom, Edie.

EDIE: Pop, don't think I'm not grateful for Marymount and everything you've done to—to shelter me. . . . But I'm staying. I'm going to keep on trying to find out who's guilty for Joey. And I'll walk home with Terry Malloy every night in the week if I think he can help.

POP: Well, I'll tell ya one thing: You ain't goin' to no more o' them crazy meetin's! That Father Barry oughta have his head examined, encouragin' ya, stirrin' everybody up like that. For what—so Runty, or Tommy, or somebody else goes to the bottom of the river?

EDIE: Pop, it doesn't have to be that way.

POP: Edie! For the sake o' yer mother, God rest her soul, you listen to me! I know the waterfront—it's something you don't mess around with . . . not if you want to stay alive!

EDIE: Pop—I'm not a child anymore. You can't scare me.

POP: The same words . . . the same words exactly! Just what Joey useta say.

Scene 11
Terry's Rooftop

REPORTER: Walkin' the waterfront, I noticed lots of pigeons circling overhead in formation. At first I thought that they were common park pigeons until I saw them return to their lofts on the tenement rooftops.

JIMMY: They're lookin' sharp now, huh Terry?

TERRY: Ya been takin' good care of 'em, matooze. Real good.

JIMMY: Ya mean it?

TERRY: I called ya "matooze," din' I? When Johnny Friendly calls ya "matooze," ye're in like Flynn.

JIMMY: Johnny Friendly—that's what he calls you? Wow. Hey—what's he say if he don't like a fella too good?

TERRY: You don' wanna hear that, ever. No sir!

JIMMY: C'mon—what's he say?

TERRY: He says "schlagoom"—an' then that fella might as well be dead.

JIMMY: "Schlagoom"?

TERRY: Don't ya ever say that word around me, kid!

JIMMY: OK, OK . . .

TERRY: Those little bastards really got it made. Eat all they want, fly around like crazy, sleep together every night, 'n' raise gobs of squabs.

JIMMY: You ain't got it so bad yaself. A big in with Johnny Friendly an' a free ticket when ya take in the fights. An' all the broads in the neighborhood puttin' out fer ya because yer name was up in lights at the Garden . . .

TERRY: Once.

JIMMY: What's the diff? The broads alla time wantin' t' feel ya muscle. You ain't got it so bad. *(Terry pushes Jimmy back and sees Edie)*

TERRY: Well, how about that . . . !

JIMMY: Who ast that broad up here?

TERRY: Go get the birds some fresh water. Move! *(Jimmy exits) (to Edie)* I din' think you'd wanna see me anymore.

EDIE: I changed my mind. I feel real "mean" tonight. *(seeing lettering on Jimmy's jacket)* The Golden Warriors . . . Are they still around?

TERRY: Hell, yes! I was their first Supreme Commander. That kid, Jimmy—he's my shadow. Thinks I'm a big man 'cause I boxed pro for a while. *(indicating coop)* The champeen flock o' the neighborhood.

EDIE: You don't mind yourself at all, do you? Joey used to race pigeons.

TERRY: He had a few birds. I got up and fed 'em this morning.

EDIE: That was really nice of you.

TERRY: I like pigeons. Send a bird five hundred miles away an' he won't stop for food or water till he's back in his own coop.

EDIE: I wouldn't have thought a person like you would be interested . . . in pigeons.

(Jimmy enters with a bucket)

TERRY: Yeah? Well, I am. You know somethin'? This city's full o' hawks. Must be twenty thousand of 'em. They perch on top o' the big hotels and swoop down on the pigeons in the park. *(makes a sound effect with his hands)* Whap!

EDIE: The poor things . . . !

JIMMY: Hawks haveta eat too.

TERRY: Watch it, kid. *(to Edie)* Hey, how d'ya like that one?

EDIE: She's a beauty.

JIMMY: She's a he. His name is "Swifty."

TERRY: My lead bird. He's always up on that top perch.

EDIE: He looks very pleased with himself.

JIMMY: Why not? He's the boss.

TERRY: Another bird tries t' take that perch, Swifty lets 'im have it. Pow!

EDIE: Oh? So even pigeons aren't peaceful.

TERRY: One thing though—they're faithful. They get married just like people.

JIMMY: Better.

TERRY: Yeah—once they're mated they stay together all their lives till one of 'em dies.

EDIE: That's nice.

TERRY: Listen—want to go out an' grab a beer?

EDIE: In a saloon . . . ?

TERRY: Dumb idea, huh? Well, how about up here? Listen, kid—go down to my place. There's a bottle o' Four Roses on the table. And beer in the fridge for chasers. Get 'em—OK?

JIMMY: OK. *(starts to exit)*

TERRY: Oh, an' kid—bring two glasses.

JIMMY: Glasses . . . ?

TERRY: Yeah, glasses. And bring up my little radio, too *(Jimmy exits)*

EDIE: Terry—were you really a prizefighter?

TERRY: Uh-huh. I was goin' pretty good for a while, too—you c'n ask anybody. But—I didn't stay in shape—an'—I hadda take a few dives.

EDIE: You mean, into the water . . . ?

TERRY: That's right—a swimmin' pool. Part of my training. Splash!

EDIE: Oh?

TERRY: Boy, are you dumb! In the ring, a dive is— *(draws a square with his fingers)*

EDIE: What are you doing?

61

TERRY: Describin' you—a square from out there. I mean you're nowhere. Miss Four Corners.

EDIE: What made you want to be a fighter?

TERRY: I had t' scrap all my life. Figured I might as well get paid fer it.

EDIE: Starting when?

TERRY: Way back—before your braids an' braces. You see, when I was just a little kid, my old man got topped off . . .

EDIE: How?

TERRY: Never mind how! Or why. OK?

JIMMY: Your order, sir. Will there be anythin' else?

TERRY: Yeah—get lost . . . *(fishing a dollar bill from his pocket)* An' take this wit' ya. *(Jimmy exits)*

EDIE: Maybe I should get lost, too.

TERRY: Aw c'mon, I didn't mean nuthin'. *(pulling some boxes up for improvised chairs)* Sit yaself down— please. Now you're beginning to live a little. *(pours whiskey)*

EDIE: I am? *(sipping her drink)*

TERRY: Not that way. Like this. Down the hatch! *(gulps)* Wham!

EDIE: *(gulps obediently)* Wham . . .

TERRY: How do you like it?

EDIE: *(almost choking)* It's quite—nice.

TERRY: This'll make it even nicer. *(hands her a beer)* Drink up.

EDIE: *(drinks and burps)* Excuse me.

TERRY: What for? How about another one?

EDIE: No, I don't think so.

TERRY: Later, maybe.

EDIE: I'm sorry about your father.

TERRY: Yeah. Anyway, me 'n' Charley was put in a place . . . they called it a Children's Home. Some home! Soon's I got big enough, I run away. Peddled papers 'n' grabbed stuff that wasn't nailed down an' got to be a club fighter. Then Charley hooked up with Johnny Friendly an' Johnny bought a piece o' me . . .

EDIE: A piece of you?

TERRY: Ferget I mentioned it. Anyway, I won about twelve straight an' then—What'm I runnin' off at the mouth for? What do you care?

EDIE: Shouldn't we care about everybody?

TERRY: What a fruitcake you are!

EDIE: Isn't everybody part of everybody else?

TERRY: Gee, thoughts! Alla time thoughts! You really believe that crap?

EDIE: Terry!

TERRY: Wanna hear my thought? Do it to him before he does it to you.

EDIE: Our Lord said just the opposite!

TERRY: I'm not lookin' t' get crucified. I'm lookin' to stay in one piece.

EDIE: I never met such a person. Not a spark of sentiment or—or human kindness in your whole body!

63

TERRY: What do they do fer ya, except get in yer way?

EDIE: And when things get in your way—or people— you just knock them aside, get rid of them? Is that your idea?

TERRY: Listen—get this straight: It wasn't my fault what happened t' Joey. Fixin' 'im wasn't my idea!

EDIE: Why, who said it was?

TERRY: Well, that Father Barry . . . I didn't like the way he kept lookin' at me.

EDIE: He was looking at everybody the same way.

TERRY: Yeah, yeah—so what's his racket.

EDIE: What are you talking about?

TERRY: You've been off in Daisyland, baby. Every- body's got a racket.

EDIE: But a priest? You don't believe in anything, do you?

TERRY: Down here, it's keepin' alive. It's standin' in with the right people so you c'n have a little loose change jinglin' in your pocket.

EDIE: But that's living like an animal.

TERRY: I'd rather live like an animal than wind up like . . .

EDIE: Like Joey? Are you afraid to even mention his name?

TERRY: You an' Father Barry. Ya never quit. Why keep harpin' on it? C'mon, drink up! Ya gotta get a little fun outa life. What's the matter with ya, anyway?

EDIE: Help me, if you can—for God's sake help me!

64

TERRY: I—I'd like to, Edie, but—there's nuthin' I can do.

EDIE: All right, all right . . . I shouldn't have asked you. *(she rises)*

TERRY: Now ye're sore at me, huh?

EDIE: What for?

TERRY: For—not bein' no help to ya.

EDIE: *(fights back tears)* If you can't you can't. But if only you'd . . .

TERRY: Edie, come on—come on . . .

EDIE: I thought I felt "mean" tonight. I'm not. I'm just . . . all mixed up.

TERRY: OK, OK. . . . Hey, maybe this'll help.

EDIE: What?

TERRY: Listen. *(turns radio on)* Hey, we got lucky— Tommy Dorsey! *(he dances a few steps comically)* You like music 'n dancin'? Ya wanna—Ya wanna spin a little?

EDIE: Up here?

TERRY: We're on! *(They dance. She dances stiffly at first, then more skillfully, as he leads her through intricate steps)* Hey, we're good! Fred and Ginger. Fred Astaire and Ginger Rogers! The Sisters oughta see you now!

EDIE: It's fun dancing with your eyes closed. I'm floating. I'm floating . . .

TERRY: I—I never knew a girl like you Edie. I always knew the kind ya just grab 'em an'—I never knew a girl like you, Edie. *(Barney enters)* Edie . . . *(they begin to kiss; Barney clears his throat)* What the hell do you want? *(turns off radio)*

BARNEY: The boss wants ya.

TERRY: Right now?

BARNEY: Uh-huh. He just got a call from Mister Big. Somethin's gone wrong, an' Johnny's hotter'n a pistol. C'mon, kid.

TERRY: I'm gonna take her home first.

BARNEY: Uh-huh. Johnny said right away. I'll see the little lady home.

TERRY: I'll come over when I'm good an' ready.

BARNEY: OK. Oney you know the boss when he gets steamed. *(exits)*

EDIE: Who's "Mister Big"? And what does Johnny want with you?

TERRY: Edie, listen, stay outa this. Quit askin' things—tryin' t' find out. Lay off—it ain't safe fer ya!

EDIE: Why worry about me? You're the one who says only look out for yourself.

TERRY: OK, get in hot water! But don't come hollerin' t' me when ya get burned!

EDIE: Why should I come hollering to you at all?

TERRY: Because . . . because . . . Listen, Edie, don't get sore now—but I think maybe we're gettin' in love with each other.

EDIE: Not me! I won't let myself!

TERRY: That goes fer me double!

GLOVER: *(from offstage)* Terry Malloy! *(enters)* Excuse me, Miss. Terry Malloy—I've been looking for you. I'm serving you with a subpoena.

TERRY: What?

GLOVER: *(takes envelope from his coat)* From the Waterfront Crime Commission. See you at the Court House—ten a.m. Friday morning.

TERRY: I told ya I don't know nuthin' an' I ain't sayin' nuthin'!

GLOVER: Bring a lawyer if you wish. And remember, you don't have to answer any questions that might incriminate you. *(puts down envelope)*

TERRY: You know what you're askin'? You're askin'—

GLOVER: We're asking you to tell the truth. Goodnight, kid. *(exits)*

EDIE: What are you going to do?

TERRY: Tell ya one thing—I ain't gonna eat cheese fer no cops, an' that's fer dam' sure!

EDIE: It was Johnny Friendly who killed Joey, wasn't it? He had him killed—or he had something to do with it—didn't he? He and your brother Charley? Isn't that true?

TERRY: Edie, listen . . .

EDIE: You can't tell me, can you? You're part of it! You're as bad as the worst of them—aren't you, Terry? You can't tell the truth!

TERRY: Edie, go back t' that school in Daisyland. You're drivin' yaself nuts—you're drivin' everybody nuts! OK? Quit worryin' about the truth alla time—worry about yaself!

EDIE: Look out for Number One. Always Number One. I should've known you wouldn't help me! Pop said Johnny Friendly used to own you. I guess he still owns you. No wonder everybody calls you a bum.

TERRY: Don't say that, Edie! Don't say that to me!

EDIE: It's true.

TERRY: I'm tryin' to keep ya from gettin' hurt. What d'ya want from me?

EDIE: More. More—a hell of a lot more! *(exits)*

(Terry stares back at her, then picks up the subpoena and glares at it. Johnny Friendly enters, and then Charley, Truck, and Barney enter.)

JOHNNY: Hey, genius!

TERRY: I—I was just on my way over t' ya, Johnny.

JOHNNY: How? By way of Chicago?

TERRY: No kiddin', Johnny, I was—

JOHNNY: Shut up, schlagoom! How many times you been knocked out?

TERRY: Only two times, Johnny. Why?

JOHNNY: It musta been once too many. Your brain's come apart. What you got up there, Chinese bells?

TERRY: Aw, Johnny . . .

JOHNNY: *(to Charley)* I thought he was gonna keep an eye on that church meeting? I thought you said he could do the job?

TERRY: Johnny, I was there. I cased the whole thing. A big nuthin'.

JOHNNY: Some operator you got yourself there, Charley. One more like him and we'll all be wearing striped pajamas.

TERRY: It was a big nuthin'! Father Barry did all the talkin'!

JOHNNY: Yeah? Well, then your goddam priest took a certain Timothy J. Nolan into a secret session with the Crime Commission and Nolan did all the talking. Now waddaya think of that?

TERRY: Runty Nolan? He don't know much.

JOHNNY: He don't huh? *(takes folder from coat)* Well, he knows thirty-nine pages of our operation.

TERRY: How'd you get that?

JOHNNY: I got it.

CHARLEY: The complete works of Timothy J. Nolan. Hot off the press. Thank Christ it was in executive session and can't be used against us until he testifies in public.

JOHNNY: Charley, you got the brains to talk, but sometimes you ain't got the brains not to talk. You know what I mean?

TERRY: Runty Nolan! I knew he had the guts—

JOHNNY: Guts! A crummy pigeon who's lookin' to get his neck wrung! *(to Charley)* You shoulda known better than to trust this punched-out bum! He was all right hangin' around for laughs. But this is business—important business—we're chopping up better'n a hunnerd G's a week. I can't afford to have meatheads fucking-up my business!

TERRY: Now listen, Johnny, how could I tell—

69

JOHNNY: I told you, shut up! You should've kept an eye on 'em—every one of them cocksuckers. You should've asked for more troops if you needed help. *(to Charley)* You realize what this means? This stuff is dynamite. And it's a state investigation—bi-state. I don't like it. I don't like this Father Buttinsky. I think it's time we got the monsignor to stick a towel in his mouth.

TERRY: Gee, Johnny, I thought I done what I was supposed—

CHARLEY: What the hell you doing with Joey Doyle's sister? It's that girl, Johnny—the little broad has him out on his feet. An unhealthy relationship.

BARNEY: Definitely!

JOHNNY: Don't see her no more. Unless you're both tired of living. Barney—get her address outa town. Now listen—if we don't muzzle Nolan, we're into the biggest stink this harbor ever seen. We got the best muscle on the waterfront. The time to use it is now—pronto—if not sooner. *(to Terry)* And ya know where you're going? Back in the hold. No more cushy job in the loft. It's down in the hold with the sweat gang till you learn your lesson. Don't make me call ya schlagoom. Now let's get the hell outa here! *(exits, followed by Barney and Truck)*

(Charley gives the hapless Terry a look, then hurries to catch up with them.)

ACT 2

Scene 1
Father Barry's Study

REPORTER: *(enters; he is outside the rectory)* The water-front may be a tough beat to cover—the boys who run it—their way—take a dim view of outsiders, especially outsiders who ask questions. News travels fast on the waterfront. You pick it up in the street—in the bars—and the latest buzz was about this young waterfront priest who was beginning to poke his nose into things he had no business looking into. *(inside, Father Barry enters carrying books)* I made a note to keep an eye on that priest. I wished I could've been a fly on the wall in the rectory where Father Pete was burning that midnight oil. *(exits)*

FATHER VINCENT: *(enters in bathrobe)* Pete, you woke me up, pacing back and forth. This is an old house—it creaks.

FATHER BARRY: Sorry, Vince—I just can't sleep. My mind's spinning like a top. Reading stuff I haven't even thought of since seminary. *(sits next to Father Vincent)* Pius the Eleventh. "Reconstruction of the Social Order"—dynamite! "Grieving for the misery and wretchedness pressing unjustly on such a large proportion of mankind, my predecessor boldly took in his own hands the cause of the workingmen—isolated, helpless, and abandoned to the hard-heartedness of employers and

71

the greed of unchecked competition. . . ." What do you think of that?

FATHER VINCENT: I think it's three o'clock in the morning and you have the early Mass.

FATHER BARRY: And I've also been reading Francis Xavier—how he stood up to the Portuguese merchants—tried to get 'em off the backs of their Hindu slaves . . .

FATHER VINCENT: Pete, that was four hundred years ago. In India.

FATHER BARRY: And things are different now, on the docks? Tell that to Johnny Friendly. Mister Sunday Catholic. Here in the front pew every week, big as life. Bigger.

FATHER VINCENT: Damn right he's big! Guess who's been in touch with Father Dowling—about you. The monsignor. It seems that the archdiocese—

FATHER BARRY: The Powerhouse.

FATHER VINCENT: —takes a dim view of your recent activities. Like getting Runty Nolan to talk to the Crime Commission. And urging other rebels to testify. Pete, you're putting Runty and the rest of 'em in jeopardy. Real danger. You've got to take the long view. Think of your career.

FATHER BARRY: I'm thinking of the men, Vince. Every one of these books tells me to do just that. And what are *you* doing? Sitting on your ass and watching good men get beaten up—killed? Jesus wasn't very partial to pharisees, Vince. He preferred good Samaritans.

FATHER VINCENT: Pete, you ever wonder why I never got a church of my own? How come I never made monsignor? Because about fifteen years ago I saw the light on my road to Damascus. Believe it or not, I was outraged at the injustice, the cruelty being done to the poor of this parish—and I spoke up for them. Too soon. Too loud.

FATHER BARRY: I'll be damned . . . !

FATHER VINCENT: *(to Father Barry)* Oh, you're not the first who tried to change things down here. You probably won't be the last, either. But change takes a long, long time. On the waterfront—and in the church.

FATHER BARRY: The men can't wait that long.

FATHER VINCENT: You mean you can't! But you have to—or you're off to Siberia. I mean it, Pete—you'll be running bingo games for the Ladies' Sodality in Schenectady. So confine yourself to the spiritual support for the Runty Nolans—moral support—

FATHER BARRY: Vince, I told him I'd stand up with him! You heard me.

FATHER VINCENT: So did the monsignor—and the cardinal.

FATHER BARRY: C'mon! The cardinal can't be backing Johnny Friendly.

FATHER VINCENT: No, His Eminence wouldn't know that thug if he fell over him. But Friendly happens to be a spear-carrier for Big Bill McCoy.

FATHER BARRY: Mister Big?

FATHER VINCENT: Who runs the Port of New York.

FATHER BARRY: I hear he owns it. Tugboats, stevedore companies, sand-and-gravel, cement . . .

73

FATHER VINCENT: And he doesn't like people who make waves. The cardinal doesn't, either—'cause McCoy's the biggest giver we ever had.

FATHER BARRY: And the biggest bastard.

FATHER VINCENT: They could squash you like a roach. And they will, Pete, unless you slow down to a walk.

FATHER BARRY: How about a *crawl?* You know, Vince, when people live together as close as we do in this rectory, they get to know each other pretty well. Maybe too well.

FATHER VINCENT: So . . . ?

FATHER BARRY: So something tells me it isn't just me you're worried about. There's a lot more—like the welfare and future of Father Vincent O'Mara.

FATHER VINCENT: All right. Look, you know what shape our pastor is in. He's on his last legs— hanging on by his fingernails. And who d' you think deserves to take over?

FATHER BARRY: So I was right: you want the job. You've been waiting a long time. You've earned it.

FATHER VINCENT: Thanks. And thanks for everything you're doing to see I don't get it. The last thing in the world we need down here is headlines about a rebel waterfront priest. And you know how the Powerhouse would handle that problem? Bring in somebody from the outside to clean house and put a cork in the bottle. Is that what you want for me—and for us?

FATHER BARRY: I hear what you're saying . . . but I think we've reached a point where we can't take one step forward—and two steps back!

74

FATHER VINCENT: You've got to be practical if you want to remain here and be effective! Then, if I'm running the show, you'll see that a few years down the road—

FATHER BARRY: Vince, I gave my word. I promised!

FATHER VINCENT: You had no right to make that promise! You're not a labor leader. You're a priest, under church discipline!

FATHER BARRY: And under the teaching of Jesus Christ and the popes who applied those teachings to help the "isolated and helpless"—like Joey Doyle and Runty Nolan!

FATHER VINCENT: Pete, you're right—but you're wrong. I just don't want you to be dead wrong.

FATHER BARRY: When Runty asked me if I'd go all the way with him, I said, yes, so help me God!

FATHER VINCENT: Now you'd better say, God help me . . . God help me!

FATHER BARRY: You say it for me, Vince.

Scene 2
The Hold of a Freighter

REPORTER: *(enters)* I was there that day, trying to blend in as usual, in the sweltering hold of an Irish freighter at dockside. The pallet was loaded with cases of Jameson's Irish Whiskey.

(Runty takes a bottle of whiskey from a crate and hands it to Luke; he then takes two other bottles and puts them

in his jacket. As Luke sings he moves to all and passes the bottle. They also pass the crate around. Terry helps with the crate.)

LUKE: Mississippi water taste like sherry wine.
Yes, Mississippi water taste like sherry wine.
North River water taste like turpentine.

(all join in)

Mississippi water taste like sherry wine.
Yes, Mississippi water taste like sherry wine.
North River water taste like turpentine.

RUNTY: *(wearing Joey's jacket, given him by Pop at the shape-up)* Who needs sherry wine? We got Jameson's! An Eye-rish ship, loaded to the gunnels with fine Eye-rish whiskey!

POP: You see, Runty, the good Lord watches over us after all.

RUNTY: When we knock off, let's have a bit of a party. We'll drink to God an' Ireland, its whiskey an' its women . . . to Joey an' Edie—and death t' tyrants everywhere!

POP: You think one bottle's enough for all that?

RUNTY: Patrick me lad, I'm aheada you. *(opening jacket and revealing two more bottles)* I was afraid one bottle might get lonely by itself. Now you see the beauty of a little man in a big coat.

LUKE: That sure is some swag jacket.

RUNTY: Joey Doyle's, rest 'im. Hey—I wonder if I c'n walk with a coupla these down my pants.

MOOSE: How many Hail Marys will the Fathers lay on you for that?

RUNTY: It'll be worth it!

TERRY: Listen, Runty—

RUNTY: *(the group breaks up)* What do you care if we rip off a coupla quarts?

TERRY: I don't. It's just that—

MAC: Come on, you guys! Get the damn thing loaded! An' don't help yaself to nuthin'! No individual pilferage!

RUNTY: Louder, Mac—I can't hear ya!

MAC: If ya kept yer ears open once in a while steada ya big mouth . . .

RUNTY: It ain't that my mouth is so big—it's just that the rest o' me is so small. *(grabs crotch)*

MAC: OK, OK—knock it off now! Stand clear! All right, take it away.

(Runty gives signal to raise pallet)

(light begins to fade as men watch pallet rise up)

REPORTER: Slowly the pallet began to rise up, out of the hold.

MORGAN: Hey, boys, wanna make some big bucks easy? The boss has a sure thing in the seventh at Belmont today. Sea Hawk—goin' off at eight to one.

TOMMY: What makes it so sure?

MORGAN: Johnny talked to the horse himself, know what I mean? You bet fifty, you get four hundred.

(Runty takes out a bottle and drinks a little, then moves)

TOMMY: Except for yer lousy twenty percent.

MOOSE: All the money I get goes home to the missus.

LUKE: Same here, J.P.

TERRY: *(looking overhead, horrified)* Runty . . . !

(Everyone screams. In blackout, sounds of whiskey crates crashing, alarm bells, and sirens. Father Barry enters and kneels next to Runty's body.)

REPORTER: I tell you it sounded like something out of hell—all that glass shattering—all that screaming—a lot o' whiskey and a lot of blood mixed together—and when the mess was cleared away, there was Runty Nolan, who always said he was on borrowed time—and finally ran out of it.

FATHER BARRY: I'm here to keep a promise. I gave Runty Nolan my word I'd stand up with him—all the way. They tell me he had the knack of getting up again and again, no matter what. But this time they fixed him good—oh, they fixed 'im, all right—unless it was an accident like Big Mac says.

MOOSE: Accident, my ass. Tell 'em, Father!

TOMMY: Give it to 'em good!

FATHER BARRY: *(stand up)* OK, boys. Some people think the Crucifixion only took place on Calvary. They better wise up. Taking Joey Doyle's life to stop him from organizing honest opposition, to stop him from testifying, that's a crucifixion. Dropping a sling on Runty Nolan because he was ready to spill his guts to the Crime Commission in public—that's a crucifixion. Every time the mob puts the crusher on a good man—tries to stop him from doing his duty as a union man and a citizen—it's a crucifixion.

78

LUKE: Speak, brother—speak!

FATHER BARRY: And anybody who lets this happen— *(to Reporter)* and I mean anybody, from the shipping companies, the Police Commissioner, and the D.A., down to the lowliest worker in the hatch—anybody who keeps silent about something evil he knows about—shares the guilt of it just as much as the Roman soldier who pierced the flesh of Our Lord to see if He was dead.

BARNEY: G'wan back to yer church, Father!

FATHER, BARRY: Pal, I'm learnin' every minute this is my church! I took a vow to follow Christ. And boys, if you don't think He's down here on this waterfront, you've got another guess coming! And who do you think He lines up with—

TRUCK: Get ahta there, Father! *(throwing banana at him)*

FATHER BARRY: *(getting hit)* I'll tell you who He doesn't line up with—He doesn't line up with hired guns!

TRUCK: Get ahta there—

TERRY: Let 'im finish!

TRUCK: Johnny ain't gonna like this . . .

TERRY: Let 'im finish!

FATHER BARRY: Every morning when the hiring boss blows his whistle for the shape-up, Jesus stands beside you. *(taunts and jeers from goons)* He sees why some of you get picked and some of you get passed over.

TOMMY: Tell 'em why, Father!

LUKE: Lay it on 'em!

FATHER BARRY: Chances are, He gets passed over Himself because He won't kick back and He won't play ball with the boys who don't have to work because they've got those strong backs of yours working for them. So Christ is left standing in the street with the other rejects. He sees the family men, worried about getting the rent money and putting food on the table for the wife and kids. And how do you think He feels when He sees them, His fellow workers, selling their souls to the mob for a day's pay? *(taunts and jeers from goons)* How does He feel when He goes to a union meeting—one of your rare, rare union meetings—and sees how it's run? Sees how few show up, and even fewer dare ask for the floor? Sees what happens to the one or two stand-up guys who haven't had the last shred of human dignity—yes, dignity in Christ!—beaten out of them?

BARNEY: Cut the bullshit, God damn you, Father!

FATHER BARRY: That's a venial sin . . . but—murder is a mortal sin!

(Barney throws beer can at Father Barry. Father Barry reacts and falls over Runty's body.)

POP: By Christ, the next bum who throws somethin' deals with me! I don't care if he's twice my size!

FATHER BARRY: *(rising)* And what does Christ think of His respectable followers, the shipping executives and the city officials who drop a fin in the basket after Mass—and then encourage and condone the goons who learned their stevedore techniques at Sing Sing and Dannemora? How does He feel about bloodsuckers picking up a longshoreman's

80

work-tab and grabbing twenty percent interest at the end of the week?

MORGAN: Keep yer nose outa my business, Father!

FATHER BARRY: What does Christ think of the easy-money boys who pose as your union leaders, and sell you out every day in the week and twice on Sunday? And wear custom-tailored suits and diamond rings on your union dues, your vocation fund, your kickback money? What must He who established the dignity of work with His own two hands think about a set-up like this? *(walks)* And how does He—who spoke up without fear against every evil *(kneels)*—feel about your silence?

TRUCK: *(to Father Barry)* How about some silence from you, shit-lips?

(Terry stops Truck with a punch in the face)

BARNEY: *(to Johnny)* You see that?

JOHNNY: Did you, Charley?

CHARLEY: Even if the Father's full of it, you don't dump on a priest. That's what the kid meant.

FATHER BARRY: You want to know what's wrong with our waterfront? It's love of a lousy buck. It's making love of a buck—the cushy job, the wholesale stealing—more important than the love of man. It's forgetting that every fellow down here is your brother—yes, your brother in Christ. But remember this, fellows: Christ is always with you—Christ is in the shape-up, He's in the hatch, He's in the union hall, He's kneeling here beside Runty Nolan. And He's saying to all of you, "If you do it to the least of Mine, You do it to Me!" You do it to Me! Believe me, boys—what they did to Joey, what they did to Runty, they're doing to you. And

81

you. And you. All of you! And only you, with God's help, have the power to knock 'em off for good! *(kneels by Runty)* OK, Runty? Amen.

Scene 3
Terry's Rooftop

TERRY: *(waving red rag on pole over his head)* G'wan, g'wan, get outa here!

EDIE: *(enters carrying a jacket)* What're you doing?

TERRY: Swifty, my favorite. Flew back three hunnerd miles. Didn't stop fer food or water—and then— would you believe it?—a damn hawk grabs him just as he's comin' in!

EDIE: Is he hurt bad?

TERRY: He's a tough bird. He c'n take it. You're gonna be OK, Swifty ol' boy. *(puts bird in box)* Gonna keep 'im in this box f' a day or two, so the other birds don't bother 'im. They're scared— that damn hawk is still up there. Smells blood, I guess. That's how they are.

EDIE: I remember Joey lost a bird that way once . . .

TERRY: I saw one torn apart—feathers all over the roof. Made me sick to m' stomach. *(takes pole and waves it again)* G'wan—get outa here, ya bastid— get outa here! *(puts pole down)* OK, Swifty—he's gone. You made it—OK? Now get some rest.

EDIE: You really love those birds, don't you? *(Terry nods)* Here, I brought this for you. *(hands him jacket)* It was Joey's.

TERRY: Aw—I'd feel funny wearin' it. Know what I mean?

EDIE: I'm not sure I do.

TERRY: Edie, lissen, there's somethin' on my mind, somethin' I gotta tell ya . . .

EDIE: Yes . . . ?

TERRY: Oney every time I try, it sticks in my throat— like somethin's caught in there 'n' I can't spit it out.

EDIE: Try, Terry. Try. *(sits)*

TERRY: Edie, I guess what I'm tryin' t' say is—I never knew a girl like you. I mean—when you're lookin' at me like you're lookin' at me now, I feel I gotta tell you that I . . .

EDIE: That you love me . . . ? *(extends her hand to him)* You don't have to say it. I know. I know . . .

(Terry turns to her, takes her into his arms, and kisses her)

Scene 4
Outside the Church

REPORTER: *(enters with newspaper)* Waterfront priest calls longshoreman's death a crucifixion! *(Father Barry enters. Reporter exits.)*

FATHER VINCENT: *(enters carrying newspapers)* A fine sermon down there, Pete. From what they say, it was one of the best . . . since Martin Luther.

FATHER BARRY: That supposed to make me feel bad, Vince? You know I don't hold with Luther any more'n you do—but at least he spoke his mind. That's all I did.

FATHER VINCENT: And you know what they're going to do? They're going to lower the boom on you, my friend.

FATHER BARRY: Vince, it took me a long time to get into this. It's too late to try an' scare me out.

FATHER VINCENT: I have to hand it to you, Pete—one word from me and you do as you damn please. You even made the *Times.* Some send-off you gave Runty Nolan!

FATHER BARRY: He deserved it. A little man with balls big enough to bowl with.

FATHER VINCENT: I'm glad you left that out. Oh, you also made the *News,* the *Mirror,* and the *Herald-Trib.* Any minute now, the afternoon papers'll be beating down the door. Precisely what we didn't need!

FATHER BARRY: I never thought it'd break like this.

FATHER VINCENT: What did you expect? You didn't spare anybody.

FATHER BARRY: I just hope it does some good.

FATHER VINCENT: I hope it doesn't do us too much harm. The archdiocese will be all over us now.

FATHER BARRY: Is that what you're worried about?

FATHER VINCENT: Damn right I am! Too loud, Pete— too soon.

FATHER BARRY: We'll see.

FATHER VINCENT: I'm afraid we will. *(exits)*

TERRY: *(from offstage)* Hold it, Father—hold it! *(enters, to Father Barry)* I want to make confession.

FATHER BARRY: Father Vincent c'n take your confession.

TERRY: But you're the one I want to tell! What you said over Runty, about keepin' silent when ya know the score . . . I'm guilty—ya hear me? I'm guilty!

FATHER BARRY: I don't want to hear it in there!

TERRY: Huh? I don't get it . . .

FATHER BARRY: Say it in the confessional and my lips are sealed. Don't you understand? I can't use it.

TERRY: But you gotta listen to me!

FATHER BARRY: Tell Father Vincent.

TERRY: Lissen—it was me set up Joey Doyle!

FATHER BARRY: Yeah? Then give it t'me straight. Fish or cut bait. Go on—there's nothing I haven't heard.

TERRY: It started as a favor—for my brother—you know, they'd ask me things, an' it's hard t' say no. A favor—who'm I kiddin'? They call it a favor but it's do it or else. An' this time the "favor" turns out t' be helpin' 'em top off Joey. I jus' thought they'd lean on 'im a little, but . . . last night with Edie I wanted t' tell her, only it—stuck in my throat. I love her, Father. She's the first nice thing that ever happened to me.

FATHER BARRY: What are you going to do?

TERRY: About Edie . . . ?

FATHER BARRY: Edie—the Commission—your subpoena. I know you got a subpoena.

TERRY: It's my own brother they're askin' me t' finger—'n' Johnny Friendly. His mother an' my mother was cousins. When I was this high he took me t' ball games an'—

FATHER BARRY: Ball games! Don't break my heart! I wouldn't care if he gave you a life pass to Yankee Stadium. You got a brother? Well, let me tell you something, kid—you got some other brothers. And they're getting the shitty end of the stick while your cousin Johnny gets mustard on his face at the ball games. If I was you— Listen, Terry, I'm not asking you to do anything. It's your own conscience that's got to do the asking.

TERRY: Conscience. . . . Never even heard the word until you 'n' Edie opened up on me. . . . This conscience stuff c'n drive ya nuts!

FATHER BARRY: It sure can, Terry. It sure can.

TERRY: Yeah, yeah—don't cost you nuthin' t' say that, over on the sidelines.

FATHER BARRY: Sidelines? Terry, you think all I did was give Runty the Last Rites? Hell, I can't stop thinkin' about what I pushed him into. The price is high. Damn high. For both of us. Good luck.

TERRY: Father—is that all ya got t' say to me?

FATHER BARRY: It's up to you, kid. One more thing— you better tell her. *(exits)*

(Edie enters)

TERRY: Edie . . . Edie . . .

EDIE: Terry—what's wrong?

TERRY: I—I been talkin' t' Father Barry.

EDIE: About us . . . ?

TERRY: About everything. It's up t' me—he says it's up t' me . . .

EDIE: What is? Terry—what's up to you? Say it!

TERRY: I told the Father . . . what I did to Joey.

EDIE: What you did . . .

TERRY: What I did to Joey. The way it was, Edie—

EDIE: Don't tell me! Don't tell me!

TERRY: —They said they jus' wanted me t' help straighten him out. So I took one o' my birds 'n' said it was his, it flew inta my coop by mistake 'n' I'd give it back on the roof. Oney Johnny's goons went up there. Jus' to work 'im over, Charley said. I—didn't know they didn't give a damn about straightening 'im out. I guess Johnny figured it was too late fer that—so they pushed 'im over . . . don't you see, Edie? I never thought they was gonna—*(Edie slaps Terry and exits)* I don't know what t' do, Edie—I don't know what t' do! I swear to God I—Edie! Edie, what'll I do? What'll I do . . . ?

Scene 5
The Friendly Bar

(Charley and Johnny are seated at a table. Morgan sits away from the table. Truck, Barney, and Mac stand.)

JOHNNY: Drink up, Charley. We're ahead of you.

CHARLEY: I'm not thirsty.

JOHNNY: That's funny. After what we been hearing about your brother, I thought your throat'd be kinda dry.

CHARLEY: So they laid a subpoena on him. That doesn't mean he's going t' talk. There's no evidence until he gives public testimony.

JOHNNY: Thanks for the legal advice, Charley. That's what I always kept you around for. Now—how do we keep him from givin' this testimony? Isn't that what you call the—er—main order o' business?

CHARLEY: Johnny, he's not the brightest, but he's a good kid. You know that.

MAC: He's a bum. After the days I give 'im in the loft—he's got no gratitude.

CHARLEY: *(rising to Mac)* You shut up! How about some gratitude to me? I kept you on the job. The boss stevedore wanted to fire you a dozen times.

JOHNNY: All right, Charley—Mac—knock it off. I'm conductin' this . . . investigation.

CHARLEY: Terry's done a few favors for us, Johnny. We mustn't forget that. It's simply that this girl and maybe the priest, too, have begun exerting some kind of influence over him that's, well, that's affecting his mental attitude. See what I mean?

JOHNNY: Mental attitude! Goddammit, talk straight so I can understand it!

CHARLEY: I mean the Doyle broad and the priest may be getting their hooks into him so deep he doesn't know which end is up anymore.

JOHNNY: I ain't interested in all that crap. We're into a bi-state investigation. This ain't no two-bit city deal we c'n talk or buy our way out of. This one is make or break. Your little brother can hang us. All I want t' know is, is he D 'n' D or is he a canary? Talk to me!

CHARLEY: I wish I knew what he is.

JOHNNY: So do I, matooze. For your sake. I was never for tying that kid in close. There's no room for fuck-ups in this business. It's time to straighten out that brother of yours.

CHARLEY: Straighten out how?

JOHNNY: OK, all you fellas—march. *(Truck, Barney, Mac, and Morgan exit)* Look, it's simple. First, you talk to him somewheres private. See if you can't get him back in line. Maybe stake him and ship 'im out. Baltimore, maybe. But if he won't play, if he tries to stiff ya—drive 'im out to . . . that place we've been usin' . . . and turn 'im over to Danny D.

CHARLEY: Johnny, you can't do that. I mean, all right, maybe the kid's out of line. But Jesus, Johnny, I can handle him. He's just a confused kid.

JOHNNY: Confused kid? Lissen, cousin—first he crosses me in public and gets away with it. Then the next joker—an' pretty soon I'm just another fella down here.

CHARLEY: But it's a risky thing, messing with a psycho like Danny D right now. Who needs it, Johnny? It's time to lie low.

JOHNNY: Don't give me that lie-low shit! I lie low now and they pile it on me. I'm a crap-shooter, Charley. When I get behind, I don't pull in. I double up on the bet. I go with everything I got. I came up that way. And, brother, I'll go down that way—if I gotta go, which I wouldn't take no bets on if I was you.

CHARLEY: Johnny, I love ya, you know that. I know the work, the guts it took to muscle-in and build this beauteeful machine. Anything you asked me, I was always there, you know that. But Johnny, this thing you're askin' here, I can't do that. I just can't do that, Johnny.

JOHNNY: Then don't. Forget I asked ya.

CHARLEY: *(getting on his knees)* Johnny, it's my kid brother. . . .

JOHNNY: If it was my kid brother—hell, if it was my own mother, God bless 'er—I'd have to do it if they crossed me. I ain't sayin' I'd like it. I'm just tellin' ya what you have to do if you wanna be a real man in this business.

CHARLEY: Jesus Christ Almighty . . . *(rising)*

JOHNNY: *(using the palm of his hand to demonstrate)* You can have it my way *(up)* or you can have it his way *(down)*. But you can't have it both ways *(rotate)*. Right? OK, deep thinker—on your horse.

Scene 6
An Abandoned Pier

(Terry is pacing nervously. He tenses up as he hears footsteps offstage.)

CHARLEY: *(enters)* Relax, kid. It's me.

TERRY: Gee, Charley, I'm sure glad ya wanted to see me. I needed to talk t' ya. What's it they say about blood, it's—

CHARLEY: Thicker than water. You wanna talk to me? First I wanna talk to you. The grapevine says you picked up a subpoena.

TERRY: That's right.

CHARLEY: Of course the boys know you too well to take you for a cheese-eater.

TERRY: Mmm-hmmm.

CHARLEY: You know, they're gettin' rather interested in your future.

TERRY: Mmm-hmmm.

CHARLEY: They think you shouldn't be on the outside so much. They want you a little more on the inside. They think it's time you had a few little things goin' for you on the docks.

TERRY: A steady job an' a few extra bucks—that's all I want.

CHARLEY: Sure, that's all right when you're a kid— but you're getting on. You're pushing thirty pretty soon, slugger. Time you got a little ambition.

TERRY: I always figured I'd live longer without it.

CHARLEY: Maybe. Look, kid—there's a slot for a boss loader on a new pier in Baltimore. I c'n fix it.

TERRY: Boss loader?

CHARLEY: Ten cents a hundred pounds on everything that moves in or out. And you don't have to lift a finger. It's five, six hundred a week just for openers.

TERRY: An' for all that dough, what do I haveta do?

CHARLEY: Absolutely nothing. You do nothing and you say nothing. You understand, don't you, kid?

TERRY: Yeah—yeah—I guess I do. . . . But there's a lot more to this than I thought, Charley. I'm telling you. A lot more.

CHARLEY: Terry—I hope you're not trying to tell me you're thinking of testifying against— Kid, I hope you're not telling me that.

TERRY: I don't know—I don't know. I tell ya I ain't made up my mind yet. That's what I wanted t' talk t' ya about.

CHARLEY: Listen, Terry—these piers we control through the local—you know how much they're worth to us . . .

TERRY: I know. I know.

CHARLEY: Then you also know Cousin Johnny isn't goin to jeopardize a setup like that for one rubber-lipped ex-tanker—

TERRY: Don't say that!

CHARLEY: —Who's walking on his heels!

TERRY: Don't say that!

CHARLEY: What the hell . . . ?

TERRY: I coulda been better!

CHARLEY: That's not the point—

TERRY: I coulda been a lot better, Charley!

CHARLEY: The point is—we don't have much time.

TERRY: I tell you, Charley—I haven't made up my mind!

CHARLEY: Make up your mind, kid! Please. Please! You think I want to take you to Three-thirty-three River Street? *(turns away from Terry)*

TERRY: Three-thirty-three—isn't that where Danny D . . . ? Charley . . . you wouldn't hand me over to Danny D . . . ? *(turns away from Charley)*

CHARLEY: *(turning to Terry and pulling a gun)* Terry! *(Terry turns to Charley)* For the last time, take the job in Baltimore. Please kid. For God's sake, I don't want to hurt you!

TERRY: Charley . . . Charley. Wow . . .

CHARLEY: I wish I didn't have to do this, Terry.

TERRY: Charley—oh, Charley . . .

CHARLEY: Please take the job.

TERRY: You know I c'd always take a punch, Charley—but this? *(pushing gun down)* Wow . . .

CHARLEY: What d'you weigh these days, slugger?

TERRY: Eighty, eighty-five. What's it to ya?

CHARLEY: Gee, when you tipped one-seven-oh you were beauteeful. You could've been another Billy Conn. That skunk I got to manage you brought you along too fast.

93

TERRY: It wasn't him! It was you, Charley. You an' Johnny. Like the night the two of youse come in the dressin' room and says, "Kid, this isn't your night—we're goin' for the price on Wilson." It ain't my night. I'd of taken Wilson apart that night! I was ready—remember the early rounds, throwin' them combinations? So what happens?—This bum Wilson, he gets the title shot—outdoors in the ball park!—and what do I get? A couple bucks an' a one-way ticket to Palookaville. I was never no good after that night. It was you, Charley. You was my brother. You shoulda looked out for me a little bit. You shoulda taken care o' me. Just a little bit. 'Steada making me take them dives for the short-end money.

CHARLEY: I always had a bet down for you. You saw some money.

TERRY: See! You don't understand!

CHARLEY: I tried to keep you in good with Johnny . . .

TERRY: You don' understand! I coulda had class. I coulda been a contender. I coulda been somebody. Instead of a bum, let's face it, which is what I am. Oh yes, I am. It was you, Charley. . . . It was you.

CHARLEY: OK, OK—I'll tell Johnny I couldn't find you. Ten to one he won't believe it, but— Go ahead, blow. Quick, Terry—and keep going . . . *(Terry exits)* Keep going . . . as far as you can.

94

Scene 7
Edie's Bedroom

TERRY: *(banging on door)* Edie, it's me! Lemme in— it's me!

EDIE: *(from her bed in darkened room)* Stop it! Stop it! Get away from there!

TERRY: I gotta see you! Gotta talk to you!

EDIE: Leave me alone. I want you to leave me alone!

(Smashing through the door, Terry bursts in)

TERRY: Edie—I had t' see you!

EDIE: Lucky Pop isn't home—he'd kill you.

TERRY: You think I stink, don't you? You think I stink fer what I done?

EDIE: I don't want to talk about it. I just want you to—

TERRY: I want you to believe me! I want to be with you.

EDIE: How can you be with Charley and Johnny Friendly and still be with me? Either way it's a lie. You've got to be one or the other.

TERRY: I don't want to hurt Charley—I don't want t' hurt you.

EDIE: You're hurting yourself. By keeping it inside you, like a poison.

TERRY: I know what you want me t' do!

EDIE: I don't want you to do anything. Let your conscience tell you what to do.

95

TERRY: That—friggin'—word—again! Shut up about "conscience"! Why d' ya hafta keep usin' that goddam word?

EDIE: I never mentioned it to you before. Never.

TERRY: No . . . ?

EDIE: You're starting to listen to yourself. That's where it's coming from.

TERRY: Yeah? I keep hearin' it—I keep hearin' it, an' I don' know what t' do . . . I don' know what t' do . . . My hand . . . I cut it on the door.

EDIE: It's just a scratch. You won't die.

TERRY: Edie . . . *(moving toward her)*

EDIE: Get away from me.

TERRY: Edie, I need ya to love me. *(taking hold of Edie)* Tell me ya love me.

EDIE: I didn't say I didn't love you. I said stay away from me.

TERRY: Edie— Edie, I—

EDIE: Stay away from me. *(she struggles; he holds her)* Stay away—*(she turns to him and hits at him; he pulls her closer)* Stay—*(they kiss and lie down together)* I love you. God help me! I love you . . . !

BARNEY: *(calling offstage)* Hey, Terry! Yer brother wants ya! He's down here.

TERRY: *(rising)* Charley . . . ?

BARNEY: He's waitin' for ya. Come on!

EDIE: No Terry—don't go. Don't go!

TERRY: Maybe Charley needs me. I better find out. *(he runs out)*

EDIE: Terry . . . ! Terry . . . ! *(grabs her coat and follows)*

Scene 8
A Riverfront Street

MUTT: *(lurching through the darkness)* Tippi-tippi-tan, tippi-tan . . .

(Charley screams offstage)

EDIE: *(enters, calling)* Terry!

JIMMY: *(enters running, followed by Truck)* Mother-fucking son-of-a-bitch! *(exits)*

TRUCK: Come here, you little shit! *(follows him off)*

MUTT: Tippi-tippi-tan, tippi-tan . . .

TOMMY: *(offstage)* Drop dead!

MUTT: Spit on me—curse me an' stone me—but I suffer fer yer sins.

TOMMY: Go suffer somewheres else, ya bum!

EDIE: *(enters)* Terry!

MUTT: I seen 'im. I seen 'im . . .

EDIE: Which way did he go?

MUTT: I seen it happen. With me own eyes I seen it.

EDIE: What? What did you see?

97

MUTT: I seen 'em put 'im to death! I heard 'im cry out!

EDIE: Who—who did you see? Tell me. Tell me!

MUTT: His executioners. They was stabbin' him in his side. Oh, I weep fer 'im . . . I weep fer 'im . . .

EDIE: Tell me who!

MUTT: Our Lord Jesus. When He dies t' save us. *(reaches out to her)*

EDIE: Oh get away—get away, you fool!

MUTT: Tippi-tippi-tan, tippi-tan . . . *(wandering off)*

EDIE: *(Terry enters and runs into Edie)* Terry—are you all right?

TERRY: Huh? Sure. Oney I can't find Charley. Charley . . . !

BARNEY: *(calling)* He's over here, Terry. Waitin' fer ya. *(exits)*

TERRY: *(Terry and Edie turn to see Charley standing. Mutt exits)* Hey, Charley . . . *(Terry and Edie cross to Charley)* Charley—you was lookin' fer me . . . ? *(Terry reaches out to Charley)* Hey, Charley . . . ! *(Terry touches Charley; Charley falls into Terry's arms, and they both go to the ground)* They topped him. They topped Charley . . . ! Scummy, mother-fuckin' bastards! He wouldn't hand me over, so—

EDIE: *(kneeling next to Terry)* Terry, let's go away!

TERRY: Charley . . .

EDIE: I mean it—let's get away from here! First Joey, then Runty, now Charley—and, any minute . . . I'm frightened, Terry—I'm frightened!

TERRY: I'll take it outa their skulls.

EDIE: I don't want to see you killed. I want to live with you—live with you. Any place it's safe to walk the streets without . . .

TERRY: I'll take it outa their skulls. I'll take this outa their skulls! *(searches Charley's pockets and finds his gun)* They put a hole in Charley. I'll put holes in them.

EDIE: No, Terry—no!

TERRY: Don't hang onto me. An' don't follow me. Don't follow me. Go get Father Barry. Tell 'im t' take care o' Charley. I don't want 'im layin' out here in this stinkin' street too long.

EDIE: Where are you going?

TERRY: Don't ask dumb questions. Just do like I say. *(getting up)*

EDIE: Terry, for God's sake! *(grabs Terry)*

TERRY: Get outa my way.

EDIE: I can't let you! I can't! You're—

TERRY: *(he shoves her aside and runs off)* Outa my way!

Scene 9
The Friendly Bar

(Bartender serving Barney and Truck. J.P. is also present.)

REPORTER: I was having a beer in Friendly's Bar when Terry Malloy walked in.

TERRY: *(enters)* I wanta see Johnny.

99

MORGAN: He ain't here.

TERRY: No? *(sits at table center)* Gimme a double.

BARTENDER: Take it easy now, Terry.

TERRY: Fuck the advice. Gimme the whiskey!

MORGAN: What'd y' do to yer mitt?

TERRY: *(downs drink)* Hit me again.

BARTENDER: Listen, Terry, why don't you just go on home before Johnny—

TERRY: No advice. Just whiskey.

MORGAN: Easy. Easy now, kid. You oughta go home an' take care o' that.

TERRY: Zip it up, J.P. I'm staying here. *(Terry pushes Morgan away)*

FATHER BARRY: *(enters followed by Luke)* Terry—don't give me a hard time . . .

TERRY: Waddaya want?

FATHER BARRY: Charley's gun.

TERRY: Mind yer own business, Father.

FATHER BARRY: This is my business.

TERRY: Go to hell!

FATHER BARRY: I want that gun.

TERRY: Go fuck yaself.

FATHER BARRY: What did you say?

TERRY: *(standing up)* I said go f—*(Father Barry punches Terry in the face. Terry falls to the ground, gets up, and lunges toward Father Barry but is stopped by Luke.)* Dammit, lemme go!

LUKE: *(pushing Terry)* You can't talk to a priest that way, you bum.

TERRY: What did you call me?

FATHER BARRY: *(between Terry and Luke)* He called you a bum. What do you think you are—a brave man, a hero? Gunning down another man isn't brave. You want to hurt Johnny Friendly? You want to fix him for what he did to Charley—and a dozen men who were better than Charley? Don't fight him like a hoodlum. That's just what he wants— He'll hit you in the head and plead self-defense.

LUKE: Right on!

FATHER BARRY: Testify tomorrow at the public hearing. Hit him with the truth. That's more dangerous to Johnny Friendly than—*(takes gun from Terry)* this little cap-pistol. That is, if you've got the guts. If you haven't, you better hang onto it. *(gives gun to Terry; turns away)* You want a beer? *(to Bartender)* Two beers. *(Bartender brings beers to the table. Terry puts gun down on table and Father Barry turns to him.)* Now you're making sense.

TERRY: Am I? To Johnny Friendly?

FATHER BARRY: To hell with him—and his boss.

TERRY: Tell Johnny I was here. *(exits)*

BARNEY: Definitely!

Scene 10
Hearing Rooms: Archdiocese and Crime Commission

(Interrogator, in a cassock, sits facing upstage, opposite Father Barry.)

INTERROGATOR: Father Barry, it has come to the attention of the Chancery Office that you not only instigated a meeting of dissident members of Local Four-forty-seven, but—

FATHER BARRY: Wait a minute! I didn't "instigate" anything. Those men are working under inhuman conditions on the docks—they were just looking for a safe place to meet. I gave it to them—I figured that's one of the things the Church has always been for: sanctuary.

INTERROGATOR: But you didn't stop with that, did you?

FATHER BARRY: I didn't see how I could.

INTERROGATOR: So you not only encouraged those men to cooperate with the Waterfront Crime Commission, you even escorted them there—

FATHER BARRY: I saw it as my pastoral duty.

INTERROGATOR: —Without waiting for official sanction from your superiors! Is that not true?

FATHER BARRY: Father, these men were being subpoenaed. With all due respect, there wasn't time for ecclesiastical red tape.

INTERROGATOR: So you just went ahead on your own, and helped them organize their testimony?

FATHER BARRY: Believe me, Father, they were rank-'n'-filers from our parish, scared to death—they needed help.

INTERROGATOR: Father Barry, comforting them in their ordeal would have been one thing—but didn't you actually take them by the hand and coach them? Take the case of Terry Malloy . . . *(on the other side of the stage a Waterfront Commission interrogator, doubled by Glover, faces Terry Molloy)*

GLOVER: Name?

TERRY: Terence Francis Malloy.

GLOVER: Do you swear to tell the truth—the whole truth—and nothing but the truth, so help you God?

TERRY: Right. I do.

GLOVER: Mr. Malloy—is it true that on the night Joey Doyle was found dead, you were the last person to see him before he fell or was pushed off the roof?

TERRY: Except for the guys who pushed him off. Believe me, Joey didn't fall—he was pushed!

GLOVER: And are you acquainted with those individuals?

TERRY: Ya mean that pair o' bums they call Specs and Barney?

GLOVER: Do you refer to Richard C. Flavin?

TERRY: That's Specs.

GLOVER: And Jackson H. Rodell?

TERRY: Yeah, that's Barney.

GLOVER: Now, Mr. Malloy, let me ask you a question regarding Michael J. Skelly, also known as Johnny Friendly . . .

(back to archdiocese)

FATHER BARRY: I still say it's my pastoral duty—that the pastoral mission of the Church obligates us to protect the workingman . . . against those who are concerned only with adding to their wealth.

INTERROGATOR: That sounds dangerously close to Marxist thinking!

FATHER BARRY: With all respect again, Father, I was quoting directly from his Holiness Pius the Eleventh. He went on to say that such people have no scruples in committing the gravest injustices against others.

INTERROGATOR: Yes, yes—we recognize the teachings of Pius the Eleventh—but how they are to be applied in this situation remains at the sole discretion of the Chaplain of the Port, who—

FATHER BARRY: Who seems to have forgotten the Christian principles of social justice!

INTERROGATOR: Your devotion to social justice is most commendable, Father—but may I remind you of the importance of balancing the demands of your own conscience against the Rule of Obedience to the authority of the church?

FATHER BARRY: Look, I wasn't only trying to satisfy my conscience by helping the men—I could see how many of them we were losing because of our failure to defend their God-given rights. And I blame that on the monsignor!

INTERROGATOR: That's enough, Father! You are restricted to the rectory of Saint Timothy's while your case is considered by the Vicar General.

(back to Waterfront Commission hearings)

GLOVER: Mr. Malloy, did the man you know as Johnny Friendly ever say anything to you about getting rid of Joey Doyle—about wanting to end his life?

TERRY: Are you kiddin'? Hell, yes!

GLOVER: Specifically, what did Mr. Skelly say with respect to Joey's death?

TERRY: Well, that he couldn't afford to let a bum like Joey—some bum!—screw 'im outa the sweet deal he had goin' on the docks. It was worth millions, see—I guess you fellas know that, huh?—so, he couldn't let Joey keep on agitatin' against 'im an' squealin' to you—he hadda scare 'im off. Anyway, that's what I thought. Oney Johnny don't play that way, he plays fer keeps. I shoulda known ya don't scare off a stand-up kid like Joey—ya kill 'im off . . . ! Goddam it, I shoulda known— Johnny kills 'em off! Like Runty 'n' Charley, an' now me maybe if he ever gets his hands on me. But I swore t' tell the truth, goddam it, and that's what you're hearin', the whole goddam truth! OK, you want more?— Just ask me!

Scene 11
Terry's Rooftop

(Terry enters—sees Jimmy on adjoining roof)

TERRY: Hiya, champ—how's the kid?

JIMMY: (hurls a dead bird at Terry) A pigeon for a pigeon! (exits)

TERRY: *(goes to coop and finds all his birds dead)* Oh Christ. Oh Christ . . . Goddam butchers! *(he sinks down, puts his head in his hands, and sobs)*

EDIE: *(enters)* I've been wanting to see you.

TERRY: Yeah? Well, ya took your time.

EDIE: Pop wouldn't let me come near you. He said it was dangerous.

TERRY: He's probably right.

EDIE: He wants me to go back to Marymount . . .

TERRY: Yeah?

EDIE: What you did at the hearing—I was so proud of you!

TERRY: Forget it. It's done.

EDIE: *(noticing dead pigeons)* Oh my God! Oh no, oh no . . .

TERRY: Every goddam one of 'em! The champeen flock of the neighborhood. *(picks up dead bird)* Even Swifty, my little champ.

EDIE: Oh Terry, why—why . . . ?

TERRY: To show me what they think of stool-pigeons, I guess.

EDIE: What do they want instead—murderers?

TERRY: Forget it.

EDIE: Terry, you've got to get away from here. Maybe ship out, or out west, a farm . . .

TERRY: Farm?

EDIE: Anywhere, as long as it's away from here, from Johnny Friendly, from the whole horrible—

TERRY: Look, the law of the waterfront is, if they're gonna get ya, they're gonna get ya. Out west—in Sing-Sing—even heard of 'em catching up with a lamster in Australia . . .

EDIE: So . . . what are you—what are we going to do?

TERRY: Don't worry about me. Go back to school. Get to be a teacher an' try t' pound some sense into a lot of snotnose kids. Maybe meet a man teacher so the two of you c'n starve to death an' live happily ever after.

EDIE: Terry . . .

TERRY: Go on! Your old man's right. I know how to duck, but I want you to go back to Daisyland lookin' as good as when you came down. Go on.

(she turns, moves off, then stops and turns back)

EDIE: Terry, I can't do it—there's no Daisyland to go back to. I want to be with you.

(They embrace, clinging to each other. Then he gently pushes her away and takes his hook from a rear loop in his jeans and drives the point into a crate.)

EDIE: What are you doing? *(he hammers his hook into crate)* You're going down there, aren't you? You think you've got to show them, don't you? That you're not afraid of them and—you won't be satisfied until you walk in and hand them your head, will you? *(Terry drives his hook into the smashed crate in mounting fury)* Then go ahead. Go and get yourself killed, you stupid, pig-headed son-of-a-bitch!

TERRY: *(picking up jacket from where it's hanging outside the coop)* Joey's jacket. Time I start wearing it. *(putting on jacket)* Everybody said I was a bum—

even you. Well—not anymore. Don't worry—I'm not gonna shoot nobody. I'm just gonna show them bums I'm not a bum no more. They don't own me no more. Don't hafta take no dives for 'em. Not in the ring. Not on the docks. Nobody owns me no more!

(Edie watches in dismay as Terry heads off)

Scene 12
Active Pier

(Longshoremen are working upstage while Johnny confers hurriedly with Mac, Morgan, and Truck.)

REPORTER: By the last shape-up I made I was finally beginning to get the ink that I had been pushing for.

JOHNNY: *(to Mac)* . . . An' here's the number you can reach me. Only fa Christ sake use a pay phone.

BARNEY: *(entering)* The car's waitin', boss. Ain't too much time.

JOHNNY: Yeah, yeah. Now listen—

MORGAN: *(hands Johnny newspaper)* This don't look good, boss.

JOHNNY: It's gonna look worse, believe me. I'm headin' for the Bahamas with Barney. I'm leavin' Mac in charge. J.P., you can go on with the loans, only lower the rates for a while, OK? Truck, you take off upstate, Canada maybe. I'll let you know when it's OK to come back. All right, Barney—

(Terry enters, wearing Joey's jacket and carrying hook)

TRUCK: Well, look who's here.

TERRY: I wan't t' talk t' you, cousin.

JOHNNY: Oh, you do? *(holding up newspaper)* About this? Read it, cheese-eater—you put it there! "Dock-Boss Tied To Three Murders"! Me! *(throws paper down)* You're a walkin' dead man! You're dead on this waterfront and every waterfront from Boston to New Orleans. You don't go nowheres, you don't drive a truck or a cab—you don't even live! You dug your grave, dead man. Go fall in it!

TERRY: Just where you put my brother! Listen, Mr. Michael J. Skelly, you're through giving orders! You wanna know somethin'? Take the heater away and y're nuthin'—take the good goods away, an' the kickbacks 'n' the shakedown cabbage away, take the pistoleros away—an' you're a great big hunk of shit! Your guts is all in yer wallet an' yer trigger finger!

JOHNNY: Go on—you're talkin y'self straight inta the river. Go on, go on . . .

TERRY: I'm glad what I done t'ya, see. You give it to Joey, you give it to Runty, you give it to Charley who was one o' yer own. You good-fer-nuthin' bum! So I'm glad what I done—ya hear me?

JOHNNY: You set me up for an indictment. I might even hafta do time. Thanks to you and yer mouth. You ratted on us, Terry!

TERRY: Listen to that shit.

JOHNNY: You ratted on us!

TERRY: From where you stand, maybe. But I'm standin' on my side now. I was rattin' on myself all them years an' I din' know it—helpin' punks like you against stand-up guys!

JOHNNY: *(taking overcoat and jacket off)* Come on—I want you. You're mine. You're mine!

TERRY: Am I? Am I? *(gives cargo hook to Luke)*

(The men gather around Terry and Johnny as they fight. Terry throws punches that drive Johnny back into Barney's arms.)

JOHNNY: Mac, yer hook—gimme! *(Mac gives Johnny his hook. Luke gives Terry his.)*

(Terry and Johnny cross hooks, and Truck steps in grabbing Terry from behind. Barney moves to Terry punching him several times in the face and stomach while Mac fends off the longshoremen. Johnny puts on his jacket and overcoat. Terry falls to the ground, and Truck and Barney stomp him.)

REPORTER: I saw that showdown between Johnny and Terry like something out of a bad dream because I knew the waterfront too well now. Johnny hadn't recruited his pistol local officers for their ability as union organizers.

POP: For God's sake stop them—stop them!

JOHNNY: He's getting just what he deserves. His days are down to minutes now.

(Truck and Barney move away as Mac moves in with a blackjack hitting Terry in the face, the second blow turning Terry over. As he is getting up, Mac strikes Terry at the base of the neck, killing him.)

TOMMY: *(rushing to Terry's body)* You took care of him, you son-of-a-bitch—took care of 'im good!

JOHNNY: It was self-defense.

POP: Bullshit! Ya topped 'im because he stood up t' ya!

LUKE: You're done for, Johnny. For good.

BARNEY: Boss, let's get ahta here!

JOHNNY: Done for huh? You think you can make this stick—this and the others? Wanna bet? I got connections, lawyers—lawyers on toppa lawyers. I'll be back, bigger'n ever, an' I'll remember ya— every fuckin' one of ya! *(Johnny exits through house followed by Barney, Truck, Mac, and Morgan. Edie and Father Barry enter and hurry to Terry's body.)*

EDIE: *(kneeling over body)* Terry . . . Terry . . . !

FATHER BARRY: *(kneeling beside Edie and Terry's body)* Oh my God . . . My God . . . *(he begins Last Rites)* Susepe Domine/Servum tuum/ancillam tuam in locum sperandae sibi salvationis a misericordia tua/Amen.

Scene 13
St. Timothy's Church Sacristy

(as Father Barry quickly dons cassock, longshoremen, Mutt, Glover, and others enter church adjoining)

FATHER BARRY: God! Day after day, forever, I'll torture myself with the question of Terry and Runty's sacrifice. I took their lives in my hands. I took these two and right or wrong I made them dare as St. Ignatius dared when he chose the Coliseum: "I am God's wheat: I am ground by the teeth of the

111

wild beasts that I may end as the pure bread of
Christ." Runty 'n' Terry 'n' all the rest of 'em—
ground by the teeth of the wild beasts in this jungle of a city. Is it all for nothin', God, or do they
get a shot at winnin', as the pure blood of Christ?
We get tired of askin', God! We're waitin' f' answers!

Scene 14
St. Timothy's Church

*(All the longshoremen there. Also, Glover and others. A
mourner begins the "Kyrie Elision." The Reporter enters,
then Father Barry enters from sacristy. Edie enters as
Jimmy follows, holding a pigeon.)*

EDIE: *(seeing Jimmy)* What do you want?

JIMMY: It's Swifty. He wouldn't die. When I went back
on the roof, he was still breathin'. I killed him
and he wouldn't die.

EDIE: Get away from me.

JIMMY: Swifty could always go the distance. A tough
old bird. Terry woulda wanted you to have 'im.
*(He gives her the bird. She takes it and sits. The Kyrie
Elision ends.)*

FATHER BARRY: Domine, dilexi decorem domus tuae,
et locum habitationis gloria tuae.

MOURNERS: *(begin piously)* O Lord, I love the beauty
of Thy house and the place where Thy glory
dwells. *(voices beginning to rise)* Destroy not my soul
with the impious, O God, nor my life with men of

112

blood. *(as the voices grow stronger and angrier, the prayer becomes a mantra of defiance)* In whose hands there is iniquity, whose right hand is full of bribes. But as for me, I will walk in my innocence, rescue me and be gracious to me . . .

MUTT: Tippi-tippi-tin, tippi-tin, tippi-tan-tippi-tan . . .

REPORTER: *(turns to audience)* Did I get the whole story into the paper? Just another rumble on the waterfront. *(stands)* How big a headline do you want for one more manslaughter case on the docks? OK, so we take it lying down. Let the mob run the waterfront arm-in-arm with the oh-so-respectable shippers. What do you want to bet, forty, fifty years from now they'll still be arm-in-arm, with the greatest natural harbor in the world still one big cookie jar—our cookie jar—with their greedy hands in it? Like Father Pete said, before they shipped him off to Schenectady, "We get tired of askin', God! We're still waitin' for answers."

(the Reporter goes to exit, stops, crosses to Mutt, gives him a dollar, and exits)